Y0-DKM-018

QUALITY IN
MARKET RESEARCH

Quality in Market Research

A Practical Guide

Peter Jackson

KOGAN
PAGE

YOURS TO HAVE AND TO HOLD

BUT NOT TO COPY

First published 1997

Kogan Page Limited
120 Pentonville Road
London N1 9JN

© Peter Jackson, 1997

The right of Peter Jackson to be identified as author of this work has been asserted by him in accordance with the Copyright, Designs and Patents Act 1988.

British Library Cataloguing in Publication Data

A CIP for this book is available from the British Library

ISBN 0–7494–20480

Typeset by Florencetype Ltd, Stoodleigh, Devon
Printed in England by Clays Ltd, St Ives plc

Contents

Preface   9

1 Introduction   **11**
The quality movement   11
Better and best   13
I know what I want (but is that what I need?)   14
Standards   16
Delivering quality   18
Process stages   20
Improving quality   22

2 Market research as an industry   **25**
What is market research?   25
The demand for market research services   28
Research suppliers   30
Market researchers   32
Trends in the market research industry   36

3 Quality and truth   **39**
Usefulness is essential but not enough   40
Market research as science   42
Positivism (and its critics) in market research   47
Qualitative research and understanding   48
Validity and reliability   50
Final words on the truth   55

4 Quality and the profession   **57**
Professions and members   57
Knowledge and professions   61
Professional organisation   63
Codes and standards   65
Professions and standards   69

Contents

Professionals and their clients   70
Is professionalism enough?   72

5   Quality and business process   **75**
Satisfying clients   75
Conformity to specification   78
Quality and money   79
Delivering market research quality through the business
process   83

6   Quality assurance and ISO 9000   **93**
What is ISO 9000?   93
The essentials of ISO 9000   96
Design   96
Meeting requirements   98
Controlling the work   99
Verification and checking   102
Solving problems   103
Management   104
Documents and records   105
Is it all worthwhile?   107

7   ISO 9000 – in more detail   **113**
ISO 9000 requirements   113
Research process requirements   114
Resources and quality data   123
Quality system control   125
The quality system circle   130
Implementing ISO 9000   132
Assessment   132

8   Standards for data collection – IQCS   **135**
Interviewing problems   135
IQCS to the rescue   141
IQCS minimum standards   142
Assessment and inspection   146
Is it all enough?   147

9   Standards for the whole research process – MRQSA   **151**
MRQSA origins   151
Scope and nature of MRQSA standards   154
Quality assurance   156
Managing the executive elements of research   158
Data collection   160
Data processing   160

Assessment	162
Implementation	164
The future of MRQSA	164
What has MRQSA achieved?	165
MRQSA approved assessment bodies	166

10 People quality – Investors in People — **167**
What is required?	167
Investors in People	172
Assessment to IiP	175
Is IiP worth having?	176

11 Quality and international research — **177**
| Quality issues in international research | 178 |
| Improving quality in international research | 180 |

12 Developing a quality system — **183**
Standards and the system	183
Quality system procedures	184
Developing procedures	188
Other documentation	196
Quality system implementation	197
Auditing	197
Assessment	198
Developing systems	199

| *Appendix: Specimen procedures* | *201* |
| *References and further reading* | *215* |

Preface

I have spent all my working life in market research; as a practitioner and later as a manager of a research business. In trying to handle the latter role, I became interested in quality issues. I also became involved in various research industry bodies where quality was very much on the agenda; AMSO, MRQSA and IQCS. My interests in both market research and quality have been the subject of books I have written in the past, but separately. I decided the time was right to bring both together in a new book and this is the result.

Who have I written for? I hope almost everyone involved in market research, whether as practitioners or users. Quality, after all, is potentially of interest to everybody in the business or on its fringes. I have also tried to make the book appeal to both those with a practical interest in implementing quality in market research and those who simply seek a better understanding of the issues.

Of course, thanks are due to the many people I have worked with over the years and especially my colleagues on the various industry bodies – AMSO, MRQSA and IQCS. In our meetings and discussions, we have wrestled with many of the ideas in this book; perhaps without always knowing that we were doing this. Thanks are also due to past colleagues at Business and Market Research, not least for having to put up with some of my obsessions over the years, as well as for permission to include some specimen procedures from B&MR's system. However, while all these thanks are due, I am solely responsible for the contents of the book which reflect my own and no 'official' view.

Peter Jackson
January 1997

1

Introduction

Quality has always been a concern of market research but only in the last few years has it become an issue – except perhaps in relation to fieldwork where attempts to improve quality, by an industry-wide approach, date back over ten years. Some of the reasons why quality has become an issue have come from within the research industry itself, but they also reflect that quality has become a consciously central concern of the wider business community.

The quality issue has been manifested in various ways in the market research world including a debate about the value of a standard for quality management – ISO 9000 (or BS 5750 as it was). There have also been new quality initiatives such as the standards developed by the Market Research Quality Standards Association (MRQSA) and the continuing development of the Interviewer Quality Control Scheme (IQCS). Among other subjects, the role and impact of these initiatives are discussed in later chapters of this book together with some practical guidance and advice on implementing formal quality schemes. However, the earlier chapters consider rather more general issues and some of the theoretical underpinning of quality in market research. First, though, in this introductory chapter, the concept of quality and how it can be achieved is discussed from a quite general perspective.

THE QUALITY MOVEMENT

Quality is in fashion and has been since the mid-1980s. By 'in fashion', I mean that quality has been a central concern of management thinking and practical application in the commercial world, with spill-over and parallels in the public sector and not-for-profit services. Anyone who has not noticed this is either immersed in something very different to the rest of us or is simply unobservant.

All sorts of reasons can be suggested for why quality has become such a central concern not only in the UK (see Callingham and Smith, 1994 for reasons why there are special reasons for concern about quality here) but throughout the economically developed world. One impetus has been the stimulus of an increasingly global economy and the effect of this on consumer expectations; if Japanese (or German etc) products are fault free, what is wrong with those made in our (UK, US etc) country? Technology also raises expectations. Back in the days of 12-inch screens and BBC-only programmes, you had to expect frequent repairs to your TV set. Valves were so unreliable. But with modern electronics you will just not tolerate any downtime in viewing. There is zero tolerance of faults. The sheer abundance of modern economies (compared with the austerity of say 40 or 50 years ago) has also created vastly higher expectations from consumers whether in the domestic or business sectors. Keeping them happy is clearly no simple matter.

These and other aspects of economic growth and expansion have all stimulated suppliers' preoccupation with quality issues. However, downturns have been a factor as well; when demand levels contract, the first need is to hang on to the customers you have and not allow competitors to take the business. Customer satisfaction in a tight business climate has been very much part of the quality 'movement'.

The existence of the quality movement is also very evident at the publication and communication level. A glance at the business shelves of any major bookshop will indicate how much has been written on the subject. There is also a whole sub-industry to spread the good news, through consultancy of all types, professional bodies, journals and many, many training programmes. Without stretching things too far, quality can be seen as a proto-religion complete with holy texts, prophets and disciples (and plenty of sinners in need of salvation). Some of the best known gurus include Deming, Crosby, Juran and Ishikawa.* Interestingly, a theme of most of these thinkers has been the impact of Japanese business success and the quality implications of this.

Business and management preoccupation with quality and the output of the quality 'industry' has been translated into formal initiatives across industries. Gaining certification to ISO 9000 (BS 5750 as was), TQM (total quality management), customer satisfaction programmes and process re-engineering have all been either part of or linked to the quality concept.

---

* See: Crosby, 1979; Ishikawa, 1985; Deming, 1989; Juran, 1989.

Nor has the softer side of management been forgotten in all this. An increased emphasis on education and training, worker motivation and 'empowerment' have all taken quality as a central organisational concern.

BETTER AND BEST

Quality has two broad and different senses. First there is quality as excellence; the best; the superb. Probably, in normal language, this usage is the more common, but as a working concept it has been either ignored or rejected by management thinkers and the quality movement. Quality as excellence, it is said, is just not a practical business concept. The second, and the more applied, interpretation is relative quality; relative that is to what is required. In other words good enough for the purpose in mind: 'fit for purpose' and better rather than the best.

Relative quality according to Crosby (1979) is:

> ... conformance to requirements. Period. We should perform the job or produce the product as we agreed to do it.

Quality then is a matter of meeting requirements with an emphasis on *customer* requirements. Providing what is wanted or (and this may be different) what is needed. A commercial qualification is made by adding the rider 'at least cost'. Practical quality is, therefore, not just a matter of giving the customer what he or she wants but doing so at least cost and most profit to the provider. However, any focus on customer wants and needs also has a very strong commercial aspect. In a competitive market this is absolutely necessary; if the customer is not satisfied he or she can always go elsewhere. Wants and needs are, however, themselves problematical in any application of quality and this will be explored shortly. For the moment though it is worth noting that if wants and needs are to be met they must be identified and understood. This is very much part of the subject matter of market research and, therefore, relative quality, whatever else, is good business for the market research industry.

In the literature of quality and in all manner of quality programmes, it is relative quality which has made the running. But quality as excellence cannot be dismissed quite so lightly and especially in relation to quality in market research. In opposition to relative quality, quality as excellence has the implication of a goal irrespective or even despite what the customer wants. If the customer does not seek excellence he or she jolly well should do so and if necessary will need to be brought up to scratch in his or her desires.

Quality as excellence resonates with concepts such as the Platonic 'Good' and 'Truth' and the latter link is of particular interest in exploring quality in market research. Whatever else, and however it is defined, the output of market research services is expected to be 'true' against some sort of absolute yardstick. In the end, few market research suppliers can be satisfied merely because the client likes the results; there is an imperative to provide 'true' findings and the practical limitations of timing and budget constraints are seen as concerning accuracy levels rather than any fundamental compromise with the concept of delivering the truth. Nor is 'usefulness' an allowable get-out. Research results might be considered useful by management as a prompt to decision making regardless of their truth but few researchers would be comfortable that the validity of their profession just rests on the ability to speed up clients' board meetings (see Collins, 1989). This subject is explored further in Chapter 3.

Quality as excellence also has a dynamic dimension. Relative quality is all very well but merely meeting current wants or needs is no stimulus to improvement. Pursuit of excellence is one way in which businesses anticipate rather than merely meet consumer demand. Innovation may also be built into quality programmes based on relative quality along with the distant drum of excellence acting as a spur.

Professionalism is also built around notions of quality as excellence. The professional–client relationship assumes less than perfect knowledge by the latter of his or her needs or wants and it is the job of the professional to deliver quality based on absolutely high standards generated from within the profession. The issue of quality and professionalism is the subject of Chapter 4.

I KNOW WHAT I WANT
(BUT IS THAT WHAT I NEED?)

I will sidestep a full discussion of the difference between wants and needs but there clearly is some distinction. In everyday speech we recognise that what we want is not always what we need and what we need may not be what we want. A basic aspect of any distinction in these terms is that 'want' is predominantly subjective whereas 'need' has a much larger objective component including technical necessity; needs have to be constrained by what can actually be achieved. Wants and needs may in fact be in conflict. To aid decision making, for example, management may want clear and unequivocal information but need true results which are intrinsically uncertain and complex. The supplier can simplify and clarify but perhaps only with some compromise of what is true. In other words, in market research (and many other knowledge based services), there is a tension between intellectual standards which are critical and uncertain but which are wrapped up in meeting client 'true' needs and commercial standards, concerned with meeting stated wants.

Nor is the problem of wants and needs only a matter of incompatibility. The need may just be mistaken or misunderstood. The client wants to solve a business issue but may be quite mistaken about the needs which market research should meet; the information sought may be irrelevant or incomplete in relation to the problem that has to be solved. The research supplier may well be under pressure to give the customer what is wanted despite what is 'truly' needed or at least choose not to consider the latter too deeply.

In some supply situations customer ignorance about true needs may be confounded by supplier ignorance about what is 'objectively' required by the client either because of a lack of effort in finding out or because of generally low levels of research and development in an industry. This does not generally apply in market research although a lack of real consensus of what constitutes 'good' research can be seen as a failure of the industry to provide for client needs. Alternatively an unscrupulous supplier may know full well what is needed but choose to offer something else; in its worst form 'ripping off' the gullible punter (again, of course, not in market research).

There are three solutions at an industry level to the problem of uncertainty and conflict between wants and needs. One is simply *caveat emptor*. It is up to the buyer to make sure of true needs and find a supplier capable of meeting these requirements. How this can be done though by the 'ignorant' buyer is not obvious except perhaps by generally promoting the virtue of scepticism. Also, it may be the case that, in time, bad suppliers – those incapable or unwilling to meet needs – are forced out of the market. However, this sort of process is often thought to work the other way round with the bad driving out the good (eg money as per Gresham's law).

The second solution to overcoming the problems associated with needs is professionalism. In this case suppliers through institutions seek to enforce adequate quality in the market by restricting the right to supply to those who are qualified and can be trusted to offer an ethical and adequate service to clients. As already mentioned, professionalism and quality are the subject of Chapter 4.

Finally, either as part of professionalism or otherwise, suppliers can be enjoined to adhere to adequate standards with the assumption that at least minimal customer needs will thereby be underwritten. Standards have become very much part of quality and are considered, separately, below as well as at various other points in this book.

Before, however, moving on from the problems of wants and needs it is worth noting that not all unsatisfied wants are grounded in any objective technical impossibility in meeting them. Wants can also be non-rational in the sense that meeting them does not 'really' contribute to meeting needs but this is not how the customer sees it. A wish for a caring service may for example be seen as more important than more objective factors in determining the outcome of patient health care. Many quality initiatives have succeeded through gaining a competitive advantage in meeting these 'non-rational' customer needs. Conversely, the market research industry is still criticised for a neglect of seemingly trivial delivery issues but which are in fact regarded as very important by clients. It may well be that 'objectively' first class research is what the client needs but it is foolish to ignore that a slick presentation adds value to the service far in excess of the extra effort involved. The output is no 'truer' but it makes the client feel more confident about the service received.

STANDARDS

Standards are a well established means of ensuring that needs in the technical sense are met. I want to be sure the fire extinguisher will work if I ever need it and assume or hope that it is produced to a standard which ensures this is the case. How the appliance works – the underlying physics – need not concern me if I can have faith in the standard and the supplier's conformity to that standard.

By far the most common quality standards in the UK are the thousands of technical product specifications issued by the British Standards Institution (BSI); there is a relevant 'BS' for virtually every significant product with a technical dimension. In much of business, buyers require their suppliers to meet relevant BS product standards as a minimum condition for being considered at all, although additional and more unique requirements may of course be specified as well. In applications which have a critical safety dimension the need for conformity to established technical standards may be also a legal or quasi-legal requirement. Two important features of technical product standards is that they concern the key parameters which determine whether or not the product works (rather than how it looks) ie whether it is 'fit for purpose' – and that conformity to the standard can be determined by objective measures and tests. If for example dimensional tolerance is part of the specification, whether this is met can be established by appropriate measurement.

While nearly all published technical standards relate to physical products, there is no reason in principle why the concept cannot be extended to various sorts of services. Again key parameters which determine whether or not the service meets basic needs can be defined and conformity objectively measured. At least this is so in principle.

One service activity where such standards have been set is education. There are now minimum standards, defined by Government, which schools are expected to meet. It is perhaps significant, however, that what such standards should be in detail and how their attainment is to be measured, has generated enormous debate. Is this because the service area is intrinsically political or because setting 'objective' standards becomes that much more difficult once we move out of the world of things which can be touched and handled?

Standards for service analogous to those in education are also found in other areas of the public sector but are less common in the commercial world and where 'standards' are spoken of they are often those of a particular supplier and applied internally within the one organisation. Proprietary standards of this type are, however, an oxymoron. Standards imply some universality, are applied by a range of organisations, not just one, and are defined by some recognised body such as the BSI or a well regarded trade association.

One very relevant case study of service standards, however, is the accountancy profession and this will be considered in more detail in Chapter 4. Here, in comparatively recent times, we have moved from a situation where there was little consistency in accountancy treatment and practice (with considerable freedom to meet clients' wants and wishes) to one where conformity to Financial Reporting Standards is effectively a legal requirement. Accountancy standards are an interesting model to consider in relation to market research but the differences in the roles and the knowledge base of the two professions must not be ignored.

A final sort of standard to mention is those developed to improve management and especially in relation to ensuring adherence to the delivery of product or service standards. First within the defence industry and later more generally it was recognised that delivering quality, whether this is defined in terms of meeting wants and needs or just conforming to defined product standards, requires a formal methodology; quality management systems or quality assurance models. Appropriate standards were, therefore, developed and published as BS 5750 which has now been superseded by the international ISO 9000 standard. As will be discussed in Chapters 6 and 7, ISO 9000/BS 5750 has had some impact within market research. Another well-established management standard is BS 7070 which addresses the management of environmental issues within a business. However, the application of this in market research is non-existent and it will not, therefore, be considered further.

Once standards are established within a field of activity the question of assessment against or to them arises. Buyers of products or services covered by standards want assurance that what is delivered is actually in conformity to the parameters set in the standard. Similarly suppliers wish to be able to demonstrate this is the case and thus differentiate themselves from 'substandard' competitors. Such assessment can be first, second or third party. First party is simply a matter of the supplier asserting that the service meets the standard. Obviously there is no harm in doing this but it may be less than convincing to the buyer (although it may be possible to seek recompense if non-conformities are subsequently found). Second-party assessment involves the buyer establishing conformity through tests in cooperation with the supplier. This may give the buyer comfort but involves much effort, not to mention inconvenience to the supplier (each major customer may wish to send in a team of quality inspectors).

A solution potentially attractive to both sides is, therefore, third-party or independent assessment. The supplier pays a recognised organisation to carry out the necessary work to determine conformity to the standard and the resulting certification can then be presented to any potential buyer requiring conformity to the standard to be demonstrated. Such third party assessment is quite well established in relation to product assessment (eg the BSI Kitemark scheme) but is even better known for the quality management standard ISO 9000. Increasingly buyers, especially in Britain, have sought assurance that their suppliers have methodologies in place to meet requirements and thus (by tautology) deliver quality. Assessment to ISO 9000 has come to be regarded as a strong indicator of this capability. There has, therefore, been some switch from a focus at the product level (with inspection of incoming material, exhaustive testing etc) to what lies behind the attainment of consistent quality levels.

Within the last ten years, the value of third-party assessment has come to be recognised within the market research industry and institutional arrangements have evolved to provide this – IQCS inspection, assessment of market research companies to ISO 9000 and very recently MRQSA – all of which are discussed in detail in later chapters.

DELIVERING QUALITY

Given that quality has become a central concern to businesses and other organisations, how is it to be achieved and delivered to the customer? Three key elements are widely recognised although the emphasis varies according to the writer, viewpoint and, arguably most important of all, the nature of the organisation seeking to deliver quality. These elements are purpose, process and people (see King Taylor, 1992).

Purpose is about commitment to quality within the organisation and this may be expressed in written mission statements, through meetings, exhortation or other ways, but however it is done it must reflect real belief and commitment and not just lip-service. Commitment must also be achieved throughout the organisation starting at the top but going all the way down. TQM programmes place strong emphasis on commitment and how to truly achieve it.

Process concerns systems and methodologies to deliver quality consistently and constantly and those stressing its importance argue that commitment, while essential, cannot deliver without the discipline and rationality of effective systems. Those with a strong emphasis on process generally favour the adoption of not only systems but formal ones and see considerable benefits in underpinning commitment with assessment to ISO 9000 (helping them to be virtuous). Developing formal systems (often seen as largely a matter of writing procedure manuals) is, however, only one, and the less radical, strand in the process approach. Another is to fundamentally reappraise all the processes which deliver product and service; to re-engineer the organisation.

Even the strongest advocates of a process approach recognise that systems work through people and quality ultimately depends on the skills and motivation of an organisation's staff. There is, therefore, a loop back to commitment. Skills may be at different levels and cover functional, management and customer service elements. Many and various approaches are offered to develop this human aspect of delivering quality. These include team building approaches, the learning organisation concept, empowerment techniques and a whole host of self-improvement panaceas some of which elevate the commonplace to profound truths, are an amalgam of doubtful psychology and in a few cases downright cranky. Changes to processes themselves of course require changes in how people work and the skills they need to employ. Similarly radical changes to processes – re-engineering – call for the same level of rethinking on the human side although where, as has been common, re-engineering has been linked to delayering, downsizing and taking out costs – polite terms for sacking half the workforce – developing any real commitment to quality must be an uphill task.

A human resource focus is always a strong element in TQM programmes and the training and skills development aspect is also covered in the UK by the Investors in People scheme promoted through Training and Enterprise Councils (see Chapter 10). UK market research companies have been among organisations buying into these approaches.

A final aspect of the people side of quality to mention at this point is professionalism (the subject of Chapter 4). Professionalism in market research, as well as in other types of knowledge businesses, is often seen as a more appropriate route to quality than an emphasis on process and systems (all well and good for rude mechanics but not for the more gentlemanly callings). The professional ethos entails induction of novices into both the necessary skills of the business and the values upheld by the profession which necessarily include quality of service to clients. There is also at least a theoretical requirement for members of the profession to continue to develop their knowledge and skills and keep abreast of all relevant intellectual development.

PROCESS STAGES

Any business involves processes which fall into broadly similar stages each of which affects the ability to deliver quality – to meet customers' wants and needs. These stages and the forms they take in market research are as follows:

Marketing

Since the subject of marketing is the identification and satisfaction of needs, it hardly needs saying that it is central to any concept of quality, although, paradoxically, quality experts have tended to ignore this vital part of the business process. It is also perhaps significant that the quality management standard ISO 9000 can be met without any consideration at all of marketing activities. This part of the business process includes identifying customers whose wants and needs can be satisfied, identifying the requirements of particular customers (in bespoke style businesses such as *ad hoc* research), developing products or services to meet the needs of a range of potential customers (eg proprietary research tools) and of course persuading customers to place business. All these activities are part of commercial market research.

Design

Not all businesses have a design element in their processes but where they do this is critical to delivering quality since it is the stage at which customer needs and wants are identified and a solution developed which is capable of meeting these requirements. The solution proposed must of course be technically viable and within the resources of the organisation. The design stage is very strongly featured in market research (or at least 'full service' work) and includes taking a brief, developing a research design (set out in a proposal) and follow-on work such as questionnaire development.

Capability

This part of the process concerns ensuring that the resources used to produce or deliver the product are capable of meeting the specification set at the design stage or otherwise agreed with the customer. In engineering, for example, there is no point agreeing a dimensional tolerance limit if the variation in milling machine output is outside this range. Capability is much less understood in market research (and not at all as this terminology) but would include skills of the professional staff, the coverage of the field-force and resources of data processing. Where deficiencies in research capability exist they can be often overcome by buying-in.

Production

In manufacturing industry, 'old time' quality management exclusively focused on the manufacturing stage with policing quality control departments and extensive inspection and testing. The equivalent to manufacturing in market research is 'doing' the research once the initial design work is complete and includes such as desk research, sampling, data collection through interviewing or qualitative techniques, data processing and analysis, interpretation and the drafting work involved in reporting. The need for care in all this and the allocation of tasks to competent staff has always been recognised in market research but more formal project management techniques have developed more slowly and more as a reaction to the growth in agency size than any recognition of its importance in quality terms. Inspection and testing has also been generally weak or at least informal except in the case of data collection where the IQCS scheme is very much concerned with effective validation of this vital link in the market research production stage. The recognition of a need for formal systems here is a direct result of the market research industry's rather chaotic structure – see the next chapter.

Delivery

Delivery is generally very strongly featured in service businesses; often 'design' and 'manufacturing' is scarcely recognised as a formal stage. Delivery is of course also present in manufacturing industry and often has a strongly physical aspect in terms of packaging, storage and transport. Many of these issues just do not arise or are trivial concerns in market research, and delivery is more a matter of effective communication of results to clients. The commercial demand for effective service as well as the availability of new, cheap technology has led to rapid developments in this part of the market research process.

After sales support

Market research largely developed as an *ad hoc* service which, in principle, ended with the delivery of the report or at least the resolution of any queries arising immediately afterwards. Research reports do not break down in the way that dishwashers do and therefore the need for formal after-sales is not understood (although the desirability of keeping-in with clients to gain repeat business is). Continuous research, however, is somewhat different in this respect and the larger companies specialising in this part of the research industry have internal structures and programmes to provide support to ongoing clients.

A final point to make about the stages and processes of market research is that unlike manufacturing and very many service businesses, very little of a tangible nature is produced. True there is a report or the material used in the presentation but the client is not paying a substantial fee just for a few dozen pages of typescript. What counts, even if it is taken for granted, is the research process behind the report and presentation and what happens here is very largely invisible to the client. It is assumed that the data provided are based on adequate methodology which has been correctly put into effect. In other words what is bought and what is critical to quality is the process itself as much as any product.

IMPROVING QUALITY

The quality concept to this point has been presented as static; organisations seek it but then just need to keep it, or to a sufficient degree. Clearly, however, this is a travesty. Organisations seek quality improvement on a continuous basis with the goal ever moving forward. The need for improvement is also, arguably, built into both concepts of quality. Quality as excellence is always unattainable and the best we can do is move a bit nearer the impossible. Relative quality is also always dynamic since the wants and needs to be fulfilled are themselves fluid and changing; in fact quality improvement is itself part of the dynamic. Improvements raise expectations.

TQM programmes take improvement as central to the whole quality issue and generally put emphasis on both the goals sought and people as the key means to make advances. The goal is often expressed as going beyond meeting customer requirements to delighting them; finding something – which may be trivial in itself – to give satisfaction over and above that which was expected and anticipated. In market research terms this may include such as how clients are handled, how information is communicated but perhaps above all the intangible creative element which lifts a routine project to something offering the client real added value.

System approaches such as those based around ISO 9000 tend to be seen by TQM proponents as at best safety chocks to quality improvements; the system stops other aspects deteriorating while specific improvements are made. At the worst, systems are said to fossilise quality and in fact inhibit innovation in customer delivery or shift the focus from substance to form. Criticisms of this sort have been quite commonly expressed in the market research industry as part of the debate about the worth of ISO 9000/BS 5750. However, this is to ignore the dynamic elements which a good quality system should include and especially the need to seek improvement through systematic and deep analysis of identified problems. ISO 9000 requires this approach although admittedly it can be and is often implemented in a purely formal and lip-service way.

Quality improvement at one level is brought about for and through meeting the needs of particular customers and clients. However, there are also more general initiatives which affect an industry as a whole and enable it better to meet the developing needs of its market. Some such initiatives in the market research field include the following.

Professional development

This covers particularly the education and training work of bodies such as the Market Research Society (MRS) but also various bodies looking at specific issues or aspects of the research industry.

Improved research tools

Research techniques and methods are continually reviewed and developed by individuals and companies but with the exception of certain proprietary 'products' these advances are made public through the professional forums and publications. As in other professions, peer group review and debate ensures that developments are validated to at least some degree.

New technology

In business generally, the application of new technology – IT is one obvious area – has been a major dynamic of quality enhancement including in areas such as product reliability and shorter and more flexible delivery schedules. Although it is an information industry, new technology had only a slow impact in market research but the pace is now quickening with developments affecting data collection (CAPI and CATI), data processing, report material production and internal management information systems. In turn this technology has impacted on the internal organisation of research companies and the overall structure of the whole industry.

Working methods and management

New technology, commercial competition and the emphasis on quality have all encouraged research companies to examine their working methods and seek improvements such as reduced fault levels and the need to re-do work; both intrinsic aspects of the quality 'movement'. There has also been the need to respond to internal growth and the change of the research industry from predominantly small businesses to at least some larger and dominant companies. An awareness of the need for project management and client handling skills is part of this change (see Smith and Dexter, 1994).

Defined minimum standards

Defined minimum standards, such as BSs, are common in many industries but have up until now made limited progress in market research and been confined to data collection (where the industry's structure created a special need) and professional codes (which imply minimum standards in some aspects of research but leave policing in practice very weak). In the last couple of years, however, real progress has been achieved through MRQSA and this will be discussed in later chapters (especially Chapter 9).

2

Market research as an industry

Having introduced quality and some quality concepts, it is time to turn to market research more specifically. This chapter describes the market research 'industry' in the UK and will be of more interest to those not familiar with how this business is organised (those who are familiar may want to skip some bits). In describing the research industry, however, I have a particular interest in showing why specific aspects of it have, for structural reasons, implications for quality issues.

Incidently I am using 'industry' to describe the practice of commercial market research because that is how it is commonly referred to. As we shall discuss in a later chapter, market research can also make reasonable claims to be a profession but practitioners tend not to describe it as such. Perhaps there is some significance in this – who has ever heard of the legal industry?

WHAT IS MARKET RESEARCH?

In terms of its application – what it is used for – market research is the provision of systematic information to assist and guide marketing decisions. Whether a company should enter a new sector, launch or modify a product, raise prices, foster a particular brand image or advertise in a specific way are all potentially decisions for which information will be needed to lessen the risk of getting it wrong. Even simple and isolated pieces of information may help in the decision process but something rather more formal and structured is what is usually meant by market research.

Within this overall framework, the specific objectives of market research projects and services are quite diverse and can be designed to meet virtually any need. Some examples include; market analysis to identify opportunities, new product development work, consumer and customer attitude research (this includes customer satisfaction survey work) and evaluating and predicting the results of changes in the marketing mix – pricing, sales methods, advertising effectiveness etc. Media research and audience measurement is virtually an industry in its own right. There is also the measurement of standards of service delivery for which some specific methods have been developed (mystery shopping) and which along with customer satisfaction surveys are very closely linked to quality concerns.

All types of industries and activities are covered by market research including industrial or business to business as well as consumer markets. Since marketing is increasingly international or global, much research work now covers a number of countries in one project. Market research techniques can also be successfully applied to public services and other not-for-profit activities with a fuzzy edge to social survey work (from which market research largely developed). One specialised form of market research is opinion polling which, although accounting for a very small share of all market research, has become the yardstick against which the reliability of market research is unfortunately (and unrealistically) measured.

The majority of market research is *ad hoc* – specific one-off projects carried out to meet the needs of a single client – but continuous surveys, which provide crucial trend data, account for some 40 per cent of the UK research spend. Often these are large-scale research programmes with the costs spread between several subscribing clients.

Market research can also be defined in terms of the methodologies used to collect the data used in marketing decision making. Primary data collection techniques are largely based on some form of interviews although forms of observation are also used (eg in mystery shopping). Figure 2.1 gives a breakdown of the importance of various forms of primary data collection used in market research.

Secondary data sources are also used, including 'traditional' desk research and its modern electronic equivalent (accessing databases and via the Internet). Continuous research also uses secondary data in the form of electronic transaction records from the tills of major retailers. Other 'impersonal' electronic data include various audience measurement techniques.

So diverse is market research that arguably the only satisfactory way of encompassing it is simply to regard it as any services that recognised market research companies carry out. However, there is one important

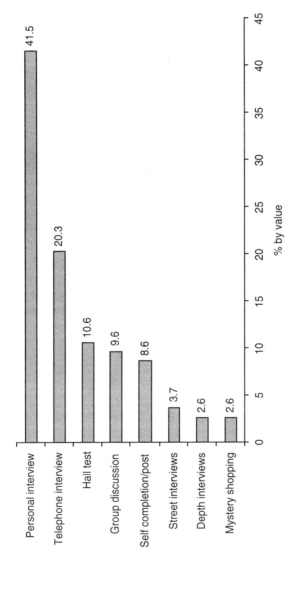

Figure 2.1 Interviewing methods as a percentage of total AMSO 1995 turnover

Source: AMSO

and overriding boundary and that is that market research aims to provide aggregated and anonymous data about consumers and markets. Businesses often wish to identify and profile individual customers and prospects and this is, of course, a quite legitimate requirement. True market research, however, for historical and ethical reasons does not provide this sort of personally identifiable information.

There is an assumption, and often an explicit promise, that information provided by survey respondents is never passed on to those who might use it as sales leads and this practice is underwritten by the professional codes of practice (and also by the form of registration usually made with the Data Protection Agency). This self-denying limitation can lead research companies into problems with 'naïve' clients and may put some real commercial opportunities off limits – eg the rapidly growing services for database marketing. It has also recently brought to the surface potential conflicts between the commercial and professional basis of market research which looks likely to be resolved eventually by making the professional code more 'realistic'.

THE DEMAND FOR MARKET RESEARCH SERVICES

A widely accepted estimate of the total value of the services provided by UK market research companies in 1995 is over £600 million. Some would suggest a higher figure (up to £1000 million) and to the turnover of research companies can be added the value of work carried out by fringe providers (eg management consultants) and of the work done in-house by organisations which are also users of the data. However, the £600 million includes the export of services by UK market research companies (over £80 million in 1995 – the UK market research industry plays 'above weight' and is large relative to the UK economy).* The fact that there is a certain vagueness in these estimates is ironical in that market researchers confidently make market size estimates for clients but seem to have difficulties when it comes to their own business. Despite its undoubted successes, however, market research, whatever its true size, is only a relatively small business sector or industry.

Figure 2.2 provides an analysis of the research spend with 'AMSO' companies by sector and is reasonably indicative of the total spend with

---

* A realistic estimate of the value of the total European market research spend in 1995 is £3800 million. The comparable figure for the US is £3500 million and for the whole world £9000 million.

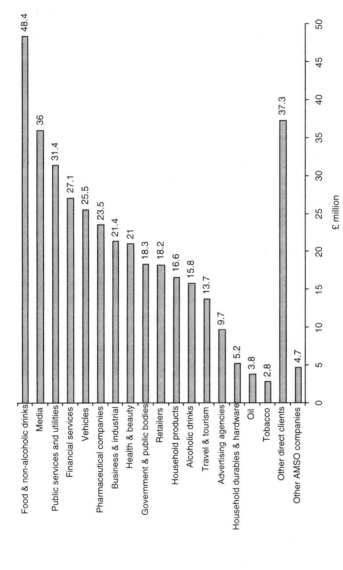

Figure 2.2 *AMSO revenue by sector (1995)*

Source: AMSO

all research suppliers. The biggest spending sector is food and drink with media research a close second. It can be inferred that most research work is carried out in consumer rather than industrial or business-to-business markets although pharmaceutical research is also carried out largely among non-domestic respondents and some of the other categories have business elements.

The companies and organisations buying research are diverse not only in terms of their own activities but also in size. However, as in most business markets, a high proportion of the total research spend is by large organisations with considerable budgets allocated to marketing activities. This includes Government (whose spend with AMSO companies is shown in Figure 2.2). Major buyers and users of market research have their own trade body – AURA (Association of Users of Research Agencies).

RESEARCH SUPPLIERS

Some primary research work is carried out 'in-house', but the very large proportion of it is carried out by commercial market research companies or agencies.* There are two trade associations of UK suppliers: AMSO (Association of Market Survey Organisations) which has about 40 member companies; and ABMRC (Association of British Market Research Companies) with over 150 members. Very broadly speaking, AMSO caters for the larger companies and only accepts 'full service' suppliers while ABMRC members are on average much smaller operations and some offer a specialised rather than full service. At the time of writing a link-up and amalgamation of these two organisations seems likely. In addition to members of AMSO or ABMRC there are many small operations (and a few larger ones) which are not members of either body and in number outweigh any double counting between the two trade bodies (some companies being members of both). Including the smallest, UK research companies exceed 300 in number with a strong geographical concentration in London and the South East (unlike in say advertising, clients based outside this area do not necessarily expect to deal with a local supplier).

Research companies follow the classic Pareto principle. Of the total 1995 turnover of £380 million for the then 33 AMSO companies, the six largest with individual turnovers over £20 million jointly accounted for around two thirds of the total, while about half of AMSO members had turnovers below £5 million (the largest – Taylor Nelson AGB – stood at £63 million). Research companies are commercial and profit-making

---

* In a literal sense 'agency' is rather misleading but I shall use it, throughout, interchangeably with research 'company'.

businesses with varied ownership patterns, although the large majority of them are privately owned by working research practitioners and in many cases the aim is to make an acceptable living for the principals rather than profit maximisation in the classic sense. However, at the top end of the pyramid it is quite common for research companies to be owned by larger groups with more ambitious commercial targets (four of the top five AMSO agencies are subsidiaries of advertising and media groups) and may be ultimately answerable to owners unconnected with the profession or its quality or ethical concerns. This is of course not to suggest that the research companies concerned are in any way unethical or any less committed to high standards; simply that the potential for structurally determined conflicts of interest can exist.

A wide range of market research services are offered, but with all agencies specialising in some way or other. One division is between those offering 'full service' and those restricting operations to just part of the research process (most commonly data collection and/or data processing). Full service work includes the quality critical process of design – identifying client requirements and developing a research programme which is adequate to meet these objectives – while restricted services such as 'field and tab' are limited to the more routine parts of the process, although with plenty of opportunities for compromising final quality of output. The two types of company often inter-trade with 'full service' companies (some of which have no internal data collection or analysis resources) providing much of the turnover of 'field and tab' operations.

Research companies also specialise in both markets and products covered and the techniques used. Few research companies take on any and every type of client although most work in quite a wide range of market sectors. There are two reasons for this. First, it is a matter of commercial advantage; generally the opportunities are greater with less sector specialisation. Second, the principles of market research are in fact much the same regardless of the product or sector covered. However, in fully understanding clients' needs and providing relevant interpretation of the data, prior experience of the product or sector has clear benefits and quality implications. Certainly, when selling-in, agencies will always emphasise such knowledge and buyers often put a premium on it.

The most common methodological specialisation is between quantitative and qualitative research. Put simply, the former is concerned to measure key marketing variables while the latter is more focused on understanding why things are as they are. Typical techniques are structured interviews with a larger and statistically significant sample of respondents for quantitative research and group discussions or a small number of depth interviews for qualitative research.

Reasons why agencies specialise in one or other of these approaches (some offer both) relate to people and resources. Professional level staff are, by training and bent, oriented to one or the other and this may include the agency principals and founders. The resources that are relevant include those for data collection and analysis. The scale of operation required in these areas is generally much greater for quantitative than qualitative research (although shortfalls can be met by subcontracting and buying-in). As a consequence most qualitative specialists tend to be small research companies down to one-man bands – economies of scale are scarcely apparent in this type of work. Other specialisations based on research techniques include companies (generally the largest) oriented to continuous research of which a distinct speciality is retail auditing and those which have developed their own proprietary research techniques. In the latter case, companies seek a competitive advantage by offering specialised techniques and models which they have developed and keep confidential and which may not as a consequence be accessible for open debate on their intellectual and practical validity. This is itself a quality issue.

Shortly, the people working in agencies are considered, but a point to make here is that while the senior staff have and certainly claim professional status, the companies as such are detached from the recognised organisation of the profession – the MRS (Market Research Society). Arguably (and this is discussed later) professionalism and the code of practice in place, is some guarantee of quality in research. However, the detachment of the companies which provide the service may in practice limit the impact of professional regulation – the professional body has very limited means of checking conformity to such as the codes of conduct and no real sanctions against companies as such (although discipline of senior members of staff is not a trivial concern to the companies). Furthermore, companies are commercial undertakings with a potential for conflict between profit goals and professional conduct. Unlike in some other professions (or at least in the classic, if outdated, concept of professionalisation), there are now fairly limited opportunities for sole professional practitioners to offer market research services to clients; the necessary scale of operations and the infrastructure needed, limit such an organisational pattern. Instead the reality is of professionals working in operations (whether as suppliers or research users) which have aims and goals outside any professional structure or concerns.

MARKET RESEARCHERS

Market research is often referred to as a people business and this is true in quite a few ways. Good research depends on flair and intellectual ability rather than machinery; whether the word processor is up to date will not affect the quality of the client's report except in the most superficial way. Similarly, placing business with an agency is often about confidence in the individual selling the project – in personal chemistry. Also, at least outside the largest agencies or specialist data processing houses, the level of capital investment required in research has been relatively low and a far more crucial issue for agency management is recruiting and keeping good staff. However, while such talented staff are vital, most people working in market research (eg interviewers) are non-professional, relatively untrained and employed in a chaotic manner. This particular structural feature gives rise to some critical quality issues.

I shall leave a discussion of whether, or the extent to which, market research is a profession until a later chapter but it is reasonable for now at least to refer to professional market researchers. Typically recruits at this level join an agency or in-house research department with a first degree from university. Rather fewer have higher degrees. The disciplines from which they are drawn are diverse; certainly a good sprinkling from the social sciences but also many with arts degrees and some having studied the natural sciences. More recently professional recruits have also come from business courses but generally the would-be researcher is not expected to have specifically relevant research knowledge, which is acquired in the first two or so 'apprentice' years through a combination of on the job training, short courses (eg as run by the MRS) and, hopefully, some self study. Depending on the subject of their first degree and mathematical skills, new recruits at a fairly early stage, gravitate to either qualitative or quantitative research.

The archetypical job for professional level staff in agencies is 'research executive' although different terms may be used depending on the company and the level of seniority achieved. However, regardless of title, the work undertaken includes much of the 'thinking' parts of the research process; taking a client's brief and identifying the requirement to be met, preparing a research design, developing questionnaires and a sampling plan, outlining the requirements from the data processing stage and preparing a report from the data including an exposition of the findings, some interpretation and very possibly conclusions drawn or inferred from the results. The research executive also has a project management role to see that the whole programme of work is carried out to specification and to timetable. This side of the work will involve liaison with the 'service' departments of the agency – data collection and data processing – and briefing staff within those areas on the specifics of the research. Finally and at least as important as the other roles, the research executive also has commercial responsibilities as well; to sell work to potential clients, liaise with them throughout the project, present the final results and control project costs.

This brief description of research executive responsibilities applies to *ad hoc* research and the agencies carrying out this sort of work. In agencies with a high level of continuous work, similar roles are carried out but with often a greater division of labour; a feature of *ad hoc* research is the wide range of tasks undertaken and low level of division of labour. Researchers were exemplars of flexible labour before the term gained common currency.

As well as research executives, professional level staff in agencies include some specialists and the managers of the service functions. The specialists are particularly involved in data analysis; from fairly routine programming or 'specing' work to the development of statistical models and other sophisticated techniques, and at both levels there is potentially a significant potential impact on the quality and validity of the final output. Service function managers are very much more concerned about people handling than intellectual activities. These managers include the heads and their assistants of outside interviewing ('field'), internal phone interviewing units and in the labour intensive process of coding and data entry. While most of the tasks which are supervised require limited formal qualifications or skills, the output of work in these areas is the foundation of the finished product, potentially prone to error and variance and for this reason the quality issues involved are both critical and problematic.

Professional level staff working in agencies are within communities which inevitably attach a high level of importance to professional research values and implicitly to quality issues peculiar to market research. People with similar training and background and professional commitment to research also work as employees of companies buying and using the research output of agencies; the client side. Often individual researchers during their career move between agencies and clients. However, not all those buying research have any real expertise and are often drawn from the more general management functions within industry, and even where professionals commission research, the output is used in decision making by managers with little understanding of how research is carried out, the status of the results or the quality issues which arise. There is, therefore, a 'laity' served by professionals whether working in-house or in an agency.

Whether of professional status or not, buyers and users of research do not work within communities where the values of research predominate. This can lead to tensions which potentially affect and diminish the quality of work supplied and used. As laity, the ultimate users of research findings may not understand the issues which affect quality of output and may for various reasons pressurise agencies to compromise on aspects of the research design or process which (the agency considers) are critical to producing work of adequate quality. This may take the form of contracting timetables to 'impossibly' short deadlines – beyond some point speed is at the expense of quality – or limiting budgets to levels which are too low to finance adequate research. There is also the policy in some organisations of buying research through competitive tendering – effectively on price alone. The quality expert Deming castigated this approach in a wider setting:

> End the practice of awarding business on the basis of the price tag. Purchasing must be combined with design of product, manufacturing and sales to work with chosen suppliers: the aim is to minimise total costs, not merely initial costs (Deming, 1989).

It is not uncommon for professional research buyers to devise all manner of stratagems to bypass their organisation's official price-first buying policy and to ensure business is actually placed with an agency thought competent to deliver quality research.

Currently, the number of professional market researchers in the UK is around 7000.* However, far more than this number earn their living through market research and the balance is taken up by various non-professional staff. Market research agencies of course employ 'generalists' such as typing and other secretarial workers, accounts staff etc – but the groups I really have in mind are data preparation staff – coders and punchers – and especially interviewers. The latter in turn split between 'field' interviewers and phone unit staff and it is the status and position of field interviewers which raise some special quality issues (although to some extent the same problems apply to these other groups as well).

In Chapter 8 the quality issues arising from field (and phone) are discussed in some detail. For the moment it is enough to mention that field interviewers are recruited without any formal qualifications, receive only limited initial training, work remotely from the designers of the research, cannot be directly supervised for more than a very small part of the time and, as essentially casual workers, commonly work for a number of agencies (sometimes even in the same week). They also have limited, if any, promotion prospects and the rates of pay offered are certainly not high by most standards – company loyalty is unlikely to be high. Even the local supervision of field interviewers is by staff who are themselves often working on a casual and freelance (if better paid) basis for more than one agency.

This structure of non-professional employment grew up in the 'cottage industry' phase of the market research industry – it still is 'cottagey' to

---

* This is based on the membership of the MRS – while some researchers would regard themselves as professional but be non-members, the MRS also includes non-practising and overseas members.

some extent – and by minimising overheads, has probably contributed significantly to the successful and long term growth of market research in the UK.* However, it is not hard to imagine that this creates some quality issues for the raw data on which any claim to research validity must rest. Problems include both variance in the administration of data collection (eg misunderstood instructions, wrong respondents, inadequate response recording) and some level of malpractice; in the extreme form made-up interviews. To attempt to address these problems the research industry responded with its own Interviewer Quality Control Scheme (IQCS) and this is discussed, as well as the underlying problems, in Chapter 8. More recently it has been recognised that the quality control approach of IQCS can sensibly be extended to other areas of the research process including professional as well as non-professional tasks and the outcome is yet another body (the market research industry, although small, has spawned numerous bodies and committees at both national and international levels). This is the Market Research Quality Standards Association (MRQSA) discussed in Chapter 9.

TRENDS IN THE MARKET RESEARCH INDUSTRY

Although by now well established, market research is still very much in a dynamic phase in both the quantitative and qualitative sense. Along with an overall increase in size has been an expansion in the range and sophistication of the services offered. Partly this has been a matter of the industry and profession developing new research tools internally and partly it has been a response to the need for businesses generally to address new types of marketing and, therefore, research problems. There is also a new emphasis on service response – itself part of the general quality movement. This has meant agencies becoming more businesslike and less 'academic'. However, this trend has its own quality tensions; service quality is a fine thing but there is a continuing need to offer research integrity and validity whether or not clients are explicitly concerned with such issues (they 'need' it whether or not they 'want' it).

An obvious structural trend of the industry is the continued growth of the larger companies and the increasing scale and complexity of their operations. One facet of this is the now quite rapid escalation of information technology (IT). The most dramatic is the increased use of CAPI

---

*   The turnover growth rates in the market research industry are the envy of many other businesses. Over 10 per cent per annum in recent years and minimally affected by recession.

(computer aided personal interviewing).* This means that interviewers record responses directly into a laptop computer or similar device instead of on a traditional paper questionnaire and then transmit data back to head office electronically rather than posted bundles of questionnaires. This offers advantages in speed and cutting out the data entry stage. There are also gains in the quality of data collection including through automatic handling of routeing and potentially lessening the opportunities to cheat. However, all this has a price and the costs of equipping a national fieldforce with CAPI are substantial and only within the budget of larger companies. Furthermore, the cost of equipping interviewers with computers and the need to use them intensively, is also likely to impact on employment structure. A full-time or at least a regular fieldforce may become preferable to the company than more flexible and casual working. If this also involves premium rates there will be an effect on smaller agencies. Such a trend could have a beneficial effect on quality of data collection through better trained and committed fieldforces.

The growth of large agencies may also impact on the working conditions and professional role of internal staff with a diminished or fragmented role for the research executive and a greater division of labour. Any decline in the numbers of 'all round' researchers will have an effect on research as a profession.

It has been argued that the growth of the largest agencies has been or will be at the expense of the medium sized company; the organisational type which is responsible for many of the established structural forms of market research and some of the problems which arise from this. However, claims that medium sized agencies will be squeezed out of business are not yet borne out by any real facts. Some medium sized agencies have continued to grow (and enter the 'big' league) and few, if any, medium sized companies have declined absolutely. At the other end of the scale new, small agencies continue to be formed. As in the past, most of these will remain small 'boutiques' but others will move up the scale.

Finally, it should be considered that not all important trends affecting market research will arise within an enclosed industry. Market research is part of a wider information service and competes to some extent with other types of providers, such as those offering database marketing and which operate with different conceptions of quality and within different ethical codes. Also, market research interacts with the whole of society in the sense that it is entirely dependent on public cooperation for its 'free' input of raw data. But such cooperation seems to be declining; response rates in surveys are falling. There are probably all sorts of reasons for this, including that research is a victim of its own success – so much

---

* The equivalent in phone interviewing, 'CATI', is rather longer established.

interviewing is carried out that potential respondents are over-fished. Also, the quality of the interview experience probably often leaves much to be desired from the respondent's perspective and this is a quality issue which professional researchers need to consider. The effect of declining cooperation and response rates may force changes in research design and practice including the greater use of past data and possibly increased data collection from panels rather than *ad hoc* samples.

3

Quality and truth

Truth or 'rightness' and the search for it, is at the heart of any concept of quality in market research; or at least it is for any concept based on excellence rather than simply meeting explicit wants. One way of expressing this is that reputable market researchers will never knowingly avoid the truth. Similarly researchers should strive to resist untruths, even if a client asks for something less than the truth to be told. Most experienced market researchers have been faced with the dilemma of a client wanting something to be 'proved' by 'objective' research but which is not completely truthful. Ethical professionals will always try and resist meeting such 'wants' and are thus arguably in breach of one type of (relative) quality.

This chapter examines the issues surrounding truth in market research. I will admit that most working market research practitioners do not concern themselves with rather abstract matters such as 'hypothetico-deductive logic' or whether positivism is a valid basis for research methodology. Nor do they need to do so. Arguably a lack of such interest is even a sign of health; engineers after all change the world dramatically without concern for the philosophical basis of their science. However, the justification for covering some of these issues is that market research is perhaps more problematic than engineering (or at least it seems so to a practising researcher) and a book on quality in market research needs for completeness, if nothing else, to at least consider the foundations on which the practice of the profession and of the industry rests. Moreover, concepts such as validity and reliability which flow from the more abstract 'truth' lead to practical quality problems which researchers need to solve in their day-to-day work.

A word of warning before moving on; the reader should not expect to find a practical guide to best methodological practice – which would be a very good way of communicating effective quality. But to do so is simply impractical. Such best practice must be considered at a level of detail including in areas such as research design, sampling methodology, questionnaire development etc, all of which justify whole books let alone whole chapters (and the literature in these areas is of course extensive). All that is attempted is to point to how some seemingly remote issues relate to problems that the good practice of the profession and industry attempts to solve.

USEFULNESS IS ESSENTIAL
BUT NOT ENOUGH

Market research is a practical activity and is financed by users who presumably believe it to be useful; there are not many other reasons for buying market research. Most researchers are probably quite content to justify their profession on the grounds that it is found useful without worrying about anything deeper. However, as mentioned in a previous chapter, the mere fact that research is believed by its clients to be useful is not justification enough. As Collins pointed out, it may be that even research with 'wrong' findings is useful in leading to some decision being made. However, such a catalytic function is only satisfactory if the information supplied not only leads to a decision being made, but enables a *better* decision to be made – compared with if the information had not been available. Therefore, research findings need in some sense to be true and right as well as useful; to *be* useful as well as *seem* useful (see Collins, 1989). However, the equally unsatisfactory nature of the converse situation needs noting; research findings may be 'true' but this will be beside the point if they are not also useful. Usefulness is essential even though it is not a sufficient justification for market research.

To be useful research has to be linked to the particular purpose it is designed to serve. Such purposes are many but all relate in some way to decision making and, of course, primarily decisions about marketing. Research is or should be commissioned because it informs some decision or other; should the product be modified, a new one launched, the price increased etc. Unlike academic research, truth for its own sake is not a reason for carrying out market research. The wisdom of spending time and money on acquiring information needs to be tested by asking what will be done with it – will it inform the decision? Will it help a better decision to be made compared with if the research was not done?

A fundamental skill in research is, therefore, relating the decisions to be made to information which will improve the chance of reaching the optimum decision. The major problem faced in this is often one of selectivity. It is not so much that there is difficulty thinking of information which might be useful but of selecting that which will be *most* useful since there will usually be neither time nor budget to cover all possibilities. Effective research requires not only competence in research itself but in understanding how its output is used in decision making. In practice the two skills do not often go together for structural reasons. Researchers are employed in agencies or at least departments remote from decision making and lack the essential background which goes into making a decision over and above any specific information input (eg the aims of the organisation, the non-marketing constraints etc). On the other hand the decision makers are 'laity' and perhaps without the skills to understand what is feasible and practical in the provision of marketing information. Decision makers may well not be research literate and researchers not experienced in practical decision making. The structural division that underlies this gap is also often reinforced by personality differences; researchers are researchers because decision making is not in their nature and decision makers lack the temperament for the nitty gritty of research detail.

These problems certainly exist and may sometimes limit the effectiveness of research. However, they should not be overstated. Useful research is (in most cases) carried out despite any structural or personality barriers. This may be achieved through informal means and long acquired experience or the researcher may follow a rather more systematic approach and develop the skills to identify needs. The decisions to be taken by the client, for example, can be regarded as linked to defined problems (eg why are sales of line 'x' declining relative to the rest of the range?) the solution of which will guide effective decision making. Even opportunities can be regarded as a sort of problem (eg is the new product formulation acceptable to existing/potential customers?).

Having in conjunction with the decision maker identified the problem or problems, hypotheses can be suggested (through creative thinking) which might explain the problem – sales of line 'x' are declining because it lacks vital product features, or is priced too high, or is poorly presented etc. A real difficulty which will be faced at this point is that the number of possible hypotheses which might explain the problem far exceed the practical resources to test and research them and some selection is essential. Such selection can be made in various ways but generally the choice will be less than the fully disinterested and objective approach supposedly required by science. It will be based on hunches, feelings, practical wisdom and other bases lacking any real rigour. Right from the start of research work, therefore, the concept of the bloodless expert does not match the reality.

Some such approach will hopefully enable a practically adequate selection of the potentially most useful information to be made. The job of the researcher is then to develop a research design capable of providing true findings within a framework of what is useful. In practice such a design is set in a research agency's proposals and part of a researcher's professional training is in how to develop adequate proposals, incorporating research designs capable of meeting the (useful) information requirement. It is worth noting, however, that proposals are also sales document and rhetoric – they must persuade as well as inform – and there is always some possibility of conflict in this duality. However they are developed, proposals and research designs should, though, provide the necessary bridge between the useful and the true and I need now to turn to the basis of truth in market research.

MARKET RESEARCH AS SCIENCE

Hardly anyone in market research would dispute that the discipline is either part of or at least linked to social science. However, how truth is arrived at through social science is a subject of still intense debate which, on the whole, is not found or found to a very much lesser degree in the natural or hard sciences. Many of the social science 'schools' are quite incompatible with each other and have mutually exclusive methods of accruing knowledge, ie radically different epistemologies.

Classic science – with physics as the paradigm – is commonalty linked to the doctrine of positivism. This is based on a number of assumptions and one basic methodology. Critics have characterised positivism as essentially a set of prohibitions against 'erroneous' methods of acquiring true knowledge (see Hammersley, 1993). The key assumptions (after Hammersley) of positivism are four in number:

1. *Phenomenalism* – things are as they seem and appear; there is no hidden essence such as Plato's 'forms'.
2. *Nominalism* – only the concrete and specific is 'real'. Abstractions and theories have their place but as tools to help us know the concrete.
3. *Value free* – value judgements and normative statements are not true knowledge and conversely, true knowledge is 'value free'. A variant is Popper's doctrine that an 'ought' cannot be derived from an 'is' (Popper, 1959).
4. *Unity of science* – the basic methodology of science is applicable to any subject area; human society is no different in principle from sub-atomic physics.

The basic method of positivism to acquire knowledge is hypothetico-deductive logic (although this method would also be advocated by other than strict positivists) and, as I shall show, this approach is certainly well represented in market research and particularly in quantitative methodology.

The hypothetico-deductive method is represented in Figure 3.1. To explain phenomena of any sort (and 'explanation' rather than 'under-standing' is the goal) the starting-point is a hypothesis in terms of a general theory which may explain some specific phenomena – eg:

> Brand leaders have a lead in terms of image greater than the lead in terms of market share held (I am making no claims that this is actually true).

On the basis of the hypothesis, a specific prediction is then made relating to concrete phenomena – eg:

> Company X (brand leader) will have a positive brand image lead over Company Y (number two) greater than its lead in terms of market share.

A test is then designed to establish whether or not the prediction is correct. In hard science this will be a controlled experiment (ie it will be known which conditions are varied and which are constant) but in the social sciences this is seldom possible and a lesser test will have to be relied on such as survey methods. If the result of the test is as per the prediction, the hypothesis, if not proven, is at least not falsified; it is provisionally true (Popper laid considerable emphasis on the concept of potential falsi-fication rather than a search for positive proof). In practice one test would hardly be regarded as adequate and another aspect of this method is replicability – it should be possible for another researcher to test the theory and show whether or not it stands up. According to positivism, science and knowledge advance by not only the accretion of tested hypotheses but by building a hierarchy of theories with those of limited scope explained by more general ones.

Before moving on the discussion, a final general point should be made about the positivist approach described; it is based on deduction from a general hypothesis to the particular – the hypothesis is not simply a generalisation from the facts. Such generalisation – induction – as a method is in fact regarded negatively in this paradigm. A legitimate question of course is how is the hypothesis formed, in the first place, if not by induction? Authorities such as Popper tend to be vague in this respect and in fact claim that how a hypothesis is thought up is of little matter. What counts is whether it is a true theory and that it is tested

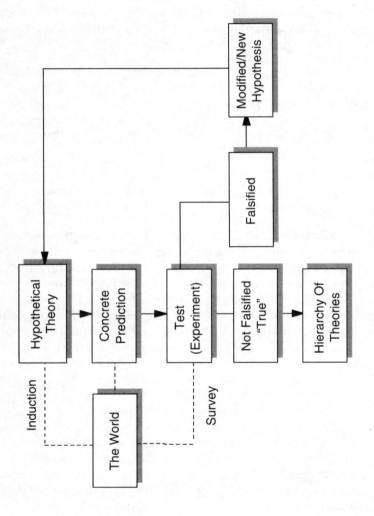

Figure 3.1 *Hypothetico-deductive logic*

empirically. Presumably, induction is at least good enough as a practical tool in hypothesis creation.

As might be imagined, positivism in social science is not without its critics and many argue that whether or not it works in hard sciences (clearly whatever the method used, hard science does work, as we all know in our daily life) it is inappropriate to all or many of the tasks undertaken in social science. Some would argue that positivism or near-positivism is in any case not the method truly followed in hard science:

> Arguments about whether social science should be like natural science no longer take place on the basis of agreement about the nature and methods of the latter (Sayer, 1992).

The criticisms are many and varied. For example, of the four basic principles of positivism it is claimed that the first two are based on naïve thinking (phenomenalism and nominalism), that value judgements (the third principle) rather than being outside true knowledge are largely the subject matter of social science and that the last (unity of science) is merely an assertion which is at least as self-evidently untrue as true.

At the heart of the anti-positive standpoint lies the issue of concepts and conceptualisation. It is argued that the social world (if not the physical world) can only be known through inevitably 'slippery' concepts – eg 'market leader', 'brand share', 'consumer attitudes' – and how these are chosen and elaborated determines all else; the findings – the information from the research – are limited to what can be fitted within the conceptual framework chosen. Additionally, social sciences concepts have 'meanings'; meanings to the observer who selects them but also very often meanings to the observed, and both draw these meanings from the social life they share. Even the language used to define the concepts is based on social life. Value free social science is, therefore, it is said, a non-starter. Also, the idea of phenomena waiting discovery in the social context is to put the reality upside down; phenomena are constructed, not found, and are intrinsically linked to the theory used to 'explain' them.

Theory (after Sayer) is also more complex than positivists allow, since as well as explanatory hypothesis, it includes conceptualisation. This covers most 'models' and 'paradigms' although these terms are also applied to hypothesis type theory – 'predictive' models invariably imply some sort of causal relationship between variables. Theory also covers various sorts of ordering frameworks – the whole of accountancy can be seen as an ordering framework as can many descriptive schemata used in social sciences.

Conceptualisation is in fact argued, by some, to be the main theoretical output of social science rather than true explanatory hypotheses which, it is said, are in fact few and far between compared with the position in the

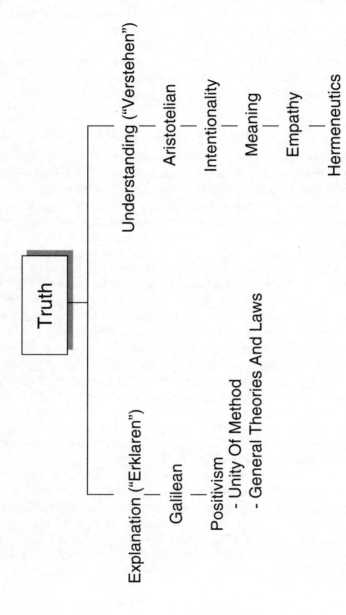

Figure 3.2 *Understanding and explanation*

hard sciences. Some claim that the only reliable general theories about society are no more than trivial commonplaces which we do not need an elaborate methodology to discover.

Even if general explanatory hypotheses can be developed in the social sciences, testing them is a rather different matter than in the natural sciences. Experimentation is generally not possible and various sorts of survey are not an equal substitute. Which variables are held constant and which are changed is nearly always problematical in any survey work. In the brand leader example it will in practice be difficult to determine whether X's position is not also due to factors not allowed for in the general theory. Another way of looking at the problem is to recognise that experimental prediction within the natural sciences is based on artificially closed systems (as contrived in the experimental design) whereas social science of necessity must work with open systems in which the pertaining conditions are inevitably uncertain. This is why reliable prediction in the social sciences is so difficult.*

Even more radically, some critics of positivism would claim that explanation as per the natural sciences should not be the aim of social science. What should be sought instead is 'inside' understanding based on meanings attached by the subjects of study; people. After Hammersley, the two approaches to knowledge can be represented diagrammatically as in Figure 3.2.

POSITIVISM (AND ITS CRITICS) IN MARKET RESEARCH

Market research – at least quantitative market research – has historically a strong positivist strain whether or not this has been consciously recognised by those adopting this position. One of the most uncompromising advocates was the late Mick Alt (see Alt and Brighton, 1981). He strongly argued for the application of a strict hypothetico-deductive methodology to such as product testing (in the article referred to, wine labelling was the example taken) or any comparable work[†] and castigated inductive methods such as 'data-dredging' (looking for relationships in the data after the event/after the survey) which were said to be a comforting approach but lacking in plausible logic. Even within the quantitative

---

* This is not to say that prediction in the 'real' natural world with contingent conditions is necessarily easier. Earthquakes are in practice as hard to predict as social revolutions.

[†] Alt did allow that purely descriptive research (that did not test theories) was legitimate although did not elaborate this point.

school of research, however, inductive logic had (and has) its defenders; Alt's position, for example, was disputed in a strongly argued riposte (see Lawrence, 1982).

If only at the level of practice – what researchers actually do – the strong positivist claims have to be regarded with some doubt. Most (the very large proportion of) market research carried out simply does not even approximate to any hypothetico-deductive methodology and induction largely rules. Data dredging approaches, for example, are how many researchers pass much of their time. However, there are other criticisms of the positivist position to consider.

One is that most research, arguably, does not even seek 'explanation'. Description is considered quite sufficient. Projects concerned with market structure analysis, user and attitude studies, customer satisfaction surveys, for example, are very largely limited to describing how things are rather than attempting to explain why they are so. Even predictive modelling is mainly 'empirical' rather than truly explanatory. Most market research is more akin to natural history than biology, but the output of such work – whether or not it 'explains' – is widely considered to be practically useful. Another point against positivism is that market research has not built up any substantial corpus of general and explanatory theory; such theory as exists tends to be at the level of conceptualisation. If, therefore, the positivist project is the right one for market research, the discipline is largely a failure. Finally, even if quantitative research in any way approximates to the positivist paradigm, qualitative research self-evidently does not and instead substitutes a quite different perspective to acquiring marketing knowledge.

QUALITATIVE RESEARCH AND UNDERSTANDING

It is perhaps significant that much of the discussion of the epistemological basis of market research has taken place within the context of qualitative rather than quantitative research. Much noise from a little chap since qualitative research accounts for less than a quarter of the value of all paid for research (although because its methods are so labour intensive it accounts for a rather higher proportion of professional time). Possibly the difference is that qualitative researchers are a more inquisitive and sensitive lot compared with smug and unreflective 'quants'. However, there is also the matter that qualitative research has often been subject to implicit attacks in respect of its claim to validity (especially over the ability to generalise qualitative findings – discussed below) and some defensive thinking has thus been stimulated.

Almost by definition, qualitative research has been concerned with explanation at some deeper level and this is often characterised as 'understanding' with a focus on meanings attached by consumers to their market experiences. Rather than ask how much more lager than bitter is consumed, or even at a simple level why one is preferred over the other, the qualitative researcher will wish to understand the symbolic meaning of lager versus bitter consumption and on this basis produce useful marketing knowledge.

Rather than positivism (which is rejected) qualitative researchers subscribe to a more 'humanistic' approach (see Colwell, 1990; Gabriel, 1990) with considerable emphasis on the researcher's softer and hands-on skills in conducting the research face to face with the subject of study. There are various schools within this general humanistic approach including; hermeneutics, semiotics, historical analysis and even post-modern market research (see Brown, 1995). A common thread is what is described as the 'linguistic turn':

> The study of language tells 20th century humans who they are ... the disciplines dealing with language and other aspects of communication hold the key to understanding human reality ... marketing research must move towards an ever greater participation in this linguistic turn (O'Shaughnessy and Holbrook, 1988).

All this is very highfalutin and it would be wrong to suggest that the average 'qually' spends his or her time worrying about such matters. In fact most will have never heard of them at all. However, that is not to say such theoretical concerns have no impact. They do, if only through a slow trickle down. Researchers may well use, say, a semiotic framework without even knowing the term. Also, most users of qualitative research will judge the outcomes in only the most fuzzy way and rely on their confidence in the practitioner. Good qualitative research is widely regarded to be that done by good qualitative researchers; it is inevitably subjective and you either accept this and its consequences or you reject all such research. One such consequence is that two first-rate qualitative researchers working to the same brief may well come up with two quite different sets of findings. However, quantitative research too has an arguably subjective element and, therefore, it is not so simple a matter as good and valid quantitative research versus shaky and dubious qualitative work.

Where has this admittedly abstract discussion taken us in seeking quality in market research? As discussed at the start of the chapter, research needs to be not only useful but also true and right. The basis of what is true is neither a simple matter nor clearcut. There is no overwhelmingly convincing model of the truth to follow and nor is there any real consensus within the market research world. Each practitioner is free to choose which tradition to follow and perhaps each has a valid contribution to make in informing marketing decisions. Whatever the case, quality (or quality as excellence) is very much to do with the truth and some particular quality issues which need to be faced in seeking truth can now be explored.

VALIDITY AND RELIABILITY

Truth in research has two components: validity and reliability, and each has a number of critical aspects. Figure 3.3 illustrates the links and is very much based on work by Collins and Sykes (Collins, 1989; Sykes, 1990).

Validity relates to the subjects of any research study and the fundamental question here is whether what we think we know about them truly corresponds to how they really are, act or think. It would be a simple matter to establish validity if we could in some way lay the observations made or measurements taken of our subjects alongside them but we cannot do this. We can only know the subjects in terms of such observations and measurements. Validity is about the truth. But in an absolute sense, what is true, over and above any observations, is unknowable. The best we can do is to increase validity through using effective tools (effective on the basis of both theory and practice) in the belief that good work comes from the successful application of these tools.

In most quantitative work the key tool is the questionnaire and maximising the design of an effective questionnaire is one of the first steps to a quality project. Questionnaires and the questions included have to both provide measures or observations relevant to the purpose of the research and capture true data from the subjects; from respondents. Both are difficult to get right and particularly the latter. The equivalent in qualitative research is the discussion guide and stimulus material although in some ways the detail is less vital because there is no intention to use these in any standard or rigorous way as there is with a quantitative questionnaire (see Cooper and Braithwaite, 1977 for a discussion of why observation errors are claimed to be lower in qualitative research, and also see Robson and Hedges, 1993).

It is often said that questionnaire design is as much an art form as a science and perhaps it is the artwork element which is often the problem. In *ad hoc* research, questions are typically made up afresh (often by quite junior executives) without any attempt to establish whether they are capable of capturing the measurement or observation sought. Basic training may have helped the designer to avoid the obvious pitfalls of ambiguous wording, two or more questions in one, leading respondents

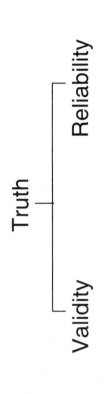

Truth

Validity

- Observation and measurement tools (e.g. questionnaires)
- Definition of subjects
- Minimisation of variability of observations and measurements (e.g. interviewer bias)
- Internal consistency of data

Reliability

- Sampling
- Repeatability
- External consistency
- In practice

Figure 3.3 *Truth, validity and reliability*

etc. But even when these basics are covered, there is still often uncertainty as to whether the data sought can actually be captured by the question or questions. Piloting, which can increase confidence, is either not done or done so superficially as to be worthless. Designing questions and questionnaires is, therefore, neither easy nor an area where the profession can believe that anywhere near the optimum is commonly attained. Guidance on this subject is, however, abundant (eg Hague, 1993). There is also much material discussing where and how things go wrong; I particularly commend O'Brien (1987) and Belson (1986).

While much has been written on the measurement and observation tools of research, there is surprisingly little apparent concern about the need to use these among relevant research subjects. It is no use having the perfect questionnaire if it is asked of respondents who have no involvement in the decisions being studied or whose attitudes or beliefs are quite irrelevant to the objectives of the research. Ask the right questions certainly, but ask them of the right people. In much research the right respondents are fairly clearcut but in some projects insufficient thought is given to the problem; pilot research may be needed to provide a valid solution before the main stage of fieldwork begins and this is seldom undertaken. Business-to-business research is an area where respondent qualification is often a special concern. In qualitative research the question of whether the respondents are 'right' is usually transparent in the groups or depth interviews* but in larger scale quantitative surveys the extent of any problem may remain hidden.

The issue of minimising variability between sets of observations – consistency in the administration of questionnaires etc – is also regarded as a more relevant issue in quantitative than qualitative research (where any minimising is through having a single moderator/interviewer both seek and interpret responses). The main extraneous variable in this case is the interviewing team; however well trained and briefed, they are people and not machines whose variance can be strictly controlled. Apart from training and briefing, validation techniques can be used to at least attempt to measure levels of variance and interviewer bias although in practice these tend to be used more to address a quite different problem; interviewer cheating. The use of IT arguably also has a positive effect on variance; interviewers using CAPI or CATI will be more likely to administer the questionnaire consistently.

A final aspect of validity is to look for internal consistency within the data from the research subjects. A simple example is that frequency of purchase, size of orders placed and annual consumption (in business

---

* Although there is the occasional problem of 'false' respondents being recruited by malpractice (see Chapter 8).

research) must all be compatible and various checks can be built into data editing work to identify consistency problems. However, the question is what is done once or if problems are found; all too often the answer in quantitative surveys is very little; not even qualifications made in the presentation of the results. Clearly any commitment to quality demands that action should be taken. In qualitative research internal consistency can be achieved by an iterative process where the moderator or inter-viewer resolves inconsistencies in the responses during the course of the interview or group.

While validity is at the level of the research subjects, reliability addresses the other major problem in arriving at the truth; on what basis can we generalise the results to a wider population – issues of inference. In quantitative research the key to this is sampling, but no such solution is generally in sight for qualitative researchers. Some qualitative researchers plead innocence of any desire to generalise, but this is nearly always disingenuous. Few clients really want to know the opinion of 20 or so housewives no matter how skilfully their deepest feelings have been probed, unless they can be taken as representatives of some wider group; all housewives, those from the C2 social class, those in the Home Counties etc. Even if the researcher does not formally permit this extrapolation it will usually be made anyway. Alternative bases for inference in qualita-tive research usually rely on some loose assumptions that, even though the sample is small, it can be taken as representative providing the measures or observations extended are not claimed to have any precision. These problems have always been the bugbear of qualitative research and, to some, imply that such methods should never or hardly ever stand alone.

I clearly cannot enter into any exposition of either the theory or prob-lems of sampling within this chapter or even book. Sampling is the basis of inference in quantitative research and the validity of any conclusions drawn from the sample data to the general population (from which the sample has been drawn) depend on the rigour of the sampling techniques used (see Rothman and Mitchell, 1989). Much research is in fact based on sampling lacking any real rigour and claims to its validity are more an act of faith than logic. Sampling is based on statistical probability theory and the necessary range of sampling error in any research has to be both recognised and taken into account in drawing research conclusions. Sampling error itself does not, however, compromise the pursuit of truth and quality. It does though necessarily qualify it.

Another aspect of inference is repeatability, coupled with stringency of testing data. If findings from research are 'true' we would expect to come up with the same results if the survey is repeated – even if by other researchers – providing of course conditions are held constant, and in practice this may be difficult to achieve. One condition that clearly cannot be held constant is time – a repeat survey by definition is carried out at a different time – and at least some types of measures or observations can be expected to change over even a short time; eg public attitudes/opinion. The mirror of this is that in continuous research or projects done in waves, we hope that differences found are the result of time and external factors rather than research variability and that is why, in these sorts of projects, a premium is put on such things as constant question wording even where doubts arise as to whether the form in use is the optimum. However, this sort of research apart, the problems of consistency, of this type, very seldom arise because while the research may be repeatable in principle, in practice it is rarely done. In comparison to hard sciences or even academic social science, the stringency of testing in market research is generally low. Some have commented (eg Sykes, 1990) that this may be a particular problem where results, as is very common, are generated by induction; the researcher examines tables and discovers an apparent relationship between variables (eg consumption levels and educational attainment) and builds firm conclusions on this basis (eg about effective promotion tools). However, for reasons argued by Alt and Brighton (1981), the relationship may be completely spurious and ought to be tested by separate research but which in practice is not undertaken for reasons of budget and timetable.

Qualitative research is frequently criticised because repeatability is not possible – even in theory. It is recognised that a different researcher, with a different perspective, is very likely to produce findings which are substantially different. However, since repeat research is not in fact a feature of *ad hoc* quantitative research either, there is no practical difference in this respect between the two forms of research.

Reliability of research output can also be tested through consistency with data from other and independent sources. Factual survey data, for example, can be compared either directly with published information or at least compatibility sought with linked data (eg the market size of a niche estimated from a survey can be compared with published estimates of a larger sector of which the niche is part). Quality of research results would be improved if this was attempted more often and with electronic access of published data it is increasingly easy to do this extra work. Consistency can also be sought where other primary research results are available. This is clearly a possibility in continuous research where big fluctuations in a reading should alert the researcher to potential survey problems, but is also possible where there are both quantitative and qualitative stages. Consistency in results at least gives comfort of the 'robustness' of the data (see Collins, 1989, for an elaboration of the robust concept).

A final approach to reliability is to consider whether the research results appear valid in the light of the outcome of any decisions they have guided;

proof through action. Since market research must be a practical discipline, validation through end results is a beguiling prospect but a path that is seldom followed. One set of problems is structural; the divorce of research users/decision makers and research providers. In much *ad hoc* research the agency simply does not know what happens next (unless it is very dramatic). Another practical point is that much research produces negative findings leading to inaction rather than action; the product is not launched, the advertising treatment not used or the market is not entered. In this situation there is usually no yardstick against which to test the research because nothing is done. The exception is the spectacularly wrong research result where someone else enters the 'no-hope' market and makes a fortune. To my shame I remember concluding from group discussion work that the home video had no future! Proprietary models – those developed as branded products by agencies – are often claimed to be validated through outcomes (see Admap, 1996). However, the 'proofs' offered are usually quite shaky.

Even where the research is followed by positive action, linking findings to subsequent events is often not easy. The research data may have been only one part of a jigsaw and perhaps only tangentially relate to the decisions taken (eg a market structure survey may have suggested possible options but these were not specifically researched before a go-decision was made). Also there is the problem of the gap between the plan and execution. The new product concept may have been valid and the basic plan sound, but the way it was launched and sold-in guaranteed a flop. Of course, if the new product is a success, the researcher will be pleased to bask in the glory, but it may all be a case of the self-fulfilling prophecy. Out of a number of alternative designs the research indicated a clear potential winner. However, its success may be no more than a matter that the marketing effort was put behind this particular design; despite the research, others may have potentially been even more successful but we will never know.

FINAL WORDS ON THE TRUTH

If this chapter has communicated anything it is hopefully that the truth and getting there is no simple matter in market research. Findings are very often uncertain and provisional. That there is no definite right answer may well be the highest quality outcome that is possible within the perspective of research as truth. However, this leads into tensions from other perspectives and especially the research user's desire for clarity and unambiguous results. 'Just tell us what to do' is the cry and the expressed need. The last thing a time-pressed marketing manager needs is a lecture on the epistemological problems of research. There are dilemmas here and complete solutions may not be attainable. There are also the inevitable compromises in research because it is carried out in a commercial framework.

As I have shown, issues of validity and reliability give rise to many real quality problems and ones which are in practice often not solved in anything approaching a satisfactory manner. These are real quality issues for the profession and industry. Commercial considerations are, however, also a major reason why the quality of some work may be questionable. The researcher knows what ought to be done for quality research but ends up compromising to meet the client's budget and willingness to spend. But research is a commercial activity (as well as a profession) and some level of such compromise cannot be avoided.

I will return to these issues, but in the next chapter I will turn to the institutional setting in which the pursuit of truth is or should be found; market research as a profession.

4

Quality and the profession

Professionalism in market research is often seen as the main underpinning of quality. Some have argued, when the need for other mechanisms has been debated, that professionalism is the *only* important means of achieving quality. My view is that the professional dimension is certainly important, but that it primarily relates to quality as excellence rather than relative quality and that even in relation to excellence, there is a need for other approaches as well. However, the professional aspect of market research and its links to quality are sufficiently important to justify a separate chapter.

There is a temptation to start the chapter with a lengthy discussion of whether or not market research is a profession in any true sense of the term but I consider such a debate to reek of the worst kind of academic pedantry. As Moore argues (Moore, 1970) an essentialist approach to defining 'true' professions is all rather futile. Instead it is more useful to see occupations lying on a continuum, at one end of which lies the long established, recognised and regulated professions (and at the other casual manual labour?). As I will describe, market research seems to lie well towards the professional end of the line.

PROFESSIONS AND MEMBERS

Professions are made up of individual members rather than corporate bodies. The Market Research Society's (MRS) members are all individuals and market research agencies as such cannot be members, though it is not uncommon to wrongly suggest otherwise (in company promotional literature). The Society can exercise no direct control over research companies. Professional bodies are, therefore, different from trade associations which do have corporate membership and which pursue commercial rather than professional interests. Where, however, as in the market research industry, both professional and trade bodies exist, there is inevitably overlap in both interests and activities and some potential for conflict; usually through the professional body impinging on the commercial interests of the trade associations. Despite overlap in the senior personnel, such conflicts surface in the UK market research industry from time to time.

Although professions are individually based and the older professions developed on an implicit and assumed commercial structure characterised by sole practitioners, most professionals, in all fields, either work in larger professional practices or as specialists in organisations whose core activities are unrelated to the particular profession. The latter structure in particular can give rise to conflicts between the requirements of the profession and the commercial ends of the organisation. This may be in relation to ethics or standards of work and quality of output. In terms of structure and the position of professional staff, market research is quite varied. Many research professionals work as sole practitioners or in very small research agencies (in numbers the large majority of agencies are small). However, more are employees of the top 20 or so agencies or work as 'clientside' research professionals. In either case, at least the potential for conflicts of ethics and quality exists.

Professions tend to seek inclusivity. They seek to ensure that all practitioners carrying out professional level work are brought into the professional fold. Once well established, professional bodies may seek to define professionals in their own field as exclusively members and stigmatise others as non-professionals and potentially 'quacks'. Problems inevitably occur, however, where the performance of the professional service depends substantially on ancillary workers. Means of overcoming these structural problems include having the ancillaries' work controlled and reviewed by full professionals (eg in legal practices) or the professionalisation of the ancillaries (eg nurses in relation to doctors). This problem certainly arises in market research with large numbers of workers responsible for key activities (especially data collection), but who are generally not fully supervised by professional workers. Neither are they organised as an ancillary profession. Amongst other issues this has some important quality aspects – see Chapter 8.

Another difficulty for professional inclusivity is specialisation. While the professional momentum is generally centrifugal, the growth of specialised branches of knowledge tends to lead in the opposite direction; to a fragmentation of practitioners pursing very different interests and activities and possibly unable to communicate to each other in any meaningful way. Specialisation certainly exists in market research – qualitative research and quantitative, *ad hoc* research and continuous, suppliers and users – but most specialisms have something meaningful and useful to communicate to and learn from each other. There are also the skilled specialists working in market research but who are not fully part of the profession (they may consider themselves to be members of other professions); statisticians and IT specialists are prime examples.

Linked to inclusivity, is the extent to which a profession is open or closed. Closed professions have rigid and demanding admittance qualifications and commonly seek to prevent non-members from offering the service. The very name of the occupation (eg solicitor, doctor etc) may be restricted or sought to be restricted to its members. Such exclusivity may even be state backed and enforced.

Open professions seek inclusivity by making entry relatively easy; based on interest and some sort of commitment rather than formal qualifications. However, the effect of this may be to reduce the standing of the profession; if anyone can join, what is membership worth? The historical trend is often to start as an open body but, once most practitioners are included, to move towards a more closed status. Achievement of such closed status, however, requires a claim to be pressed and accepted by the client base and wider public, that the profession has some special knowledge which is necessary to deliver the service to an adequate level of quality. Market research has succeeded to only a limited degree in such claims.

One strategy along the way to closed status is to develop grades of membership such as full and associate, with only full members recognised as the 'real' professionals and to restrict voting rights in the organisation accordingly. The MRS has adopted this approach and has recently formalised the basis of its full members.

While closed professions may welcome some aspects of state involvement and especially where it effectively grants a monopoly of practice to members of the profession, regulation of how the professionals perform their work is invariably strongly resisted. Indeed self-regulation by committed members is usually part of claimed professional status and imposed outside control is commonly seen as a failure of the professional institutions (eg teaching). State regulation tends to be most evident where it is considered that the life and health of the professions' clients might be at risk, but risks to wealth are also an excuse for intervention (eg the financial services industry, although this is not in any sense a unified profession). There is no direct state regulation or involvement in the market research profession* or any pressure for this to happen. Market research services do affect the wealth of clients, but of corporate bodies (which rightly or wrongly are assumed to be informed clients) rather than individuals.

Being a professional is supposed to involve more than merely following an occupation or earning an income; a profession is supposed to be a 'calling'. A calling has obvious religious connotations and links to the clergy (which was one of the historic professions). It implies that the individual would want to pursue the activity regardless of reward. In point of fact this is clearly not the case today; people become professionals to enhance their income, not restrict it. Market research is also unlikely to be carried out purely out of a love of the subject or for humanity's sake. However, the concept of a calling still has some force and implies that even though members of the profession may earn lucrative salaries, reward is in the context of commitment to norms and standards set by the profession. A professional is expected not to be willing to do anything for money even if it is allowed within the framework of the general law. These restrictions are supposed to protect clients and provide some guarantee of quality; professionals are expected to deliver the best and the true or at least strive to do so. This sense of calling is implicitly recognised within market research.

The ethics and standards of a profession relate to dealings with each other as much as the outside world. Members of a profession are meant to be a 'brotherhood' and distinct from the outside laity. As brothers (or sisters), members are expected to deal with each other fairly and with consideration even where they are commercially in competition. In the past professions have tended to ban 'vulgar' forms of competition between members with such as restrictions on advertising and protocols for taking on another professional's clients. These restrictions have, however, tended to be relaxed as a result of external pressures and because more junior members have come to realise that the restrictions serve to protect the interests of the well established as much as, or more than, clients. This leads to the point that brotherhood within professions has its critics. It is all very well for members to respect each other but are the interests of their clients as well served? In this sense professions, it is argued, stand in the way of client service and may become (or have always been) selfserving conspiracies. One does not have to go as far as Ivan Illich who regards professions as 'disabling' (Illich, 1977) to recognise ways in which professional structures and rules do not always serve clients'

---

* Market research of course operates within the general law and some legal requirements are particularly relevent eg the Data Protection Act. However, such laws were not passed specifically to regulate market research.

best interests. Within market research there has been little reported evidence of this although I am sure it is present to some degree (eg see Lewis, 1988). Arguably, a major factor limiting any self-serving tendency within market research is that it is not well enough regarded and respected by its client base for the profession to get above itself. It is also still an open profession and subject to 'outside' competition.

KNOWLEDGE AND PROFESSIONS

Professions are all knowledge based; what the professional has to offer is his or her expertise. Nor is this knowledge a mere collection of practical techniques; it cannot be set out recipe-style in a 'cookbook'. On the contrary, 'full' professional knowledge, while obviously applied, is underpinned by a theoretical body of knowledge and usually intertwined with academic fields of study – some professions explicitly claim to be 'learned'. Possibly not all practitioners are as well versed as they might be in the full depth of knowledge, but the profession as a whole has roots which can be tapped as required and which have a constant interchange with practical applications. In part this deeper knowledge of what is 'true' defines what is quality in a professional market research service.

I have, in the previous chapter, explored some of the theoretical roots of market research in social science and shown that they clearly exist even if they are contentious in part. There is also a distinct academic and practical literature on market research through journals and other publications in both the UK and worldwide. The market research professional bodies also provide forums for the exchange and advancement of knowledge and some long-term projects (eg through the work of the Research Development Foundation in the UK). As in other professions, there is commitment to not only have a basis in knowledge but also to advance knowledge. There is an assumption of improvement and, therefore, a striving for quality. Professions are more than learned societies but they have this aspect to their institutional structures and in this way link into the wider intellectual world (eg to university departments).

Because knowledge is at the core of their claims to special status, professions take education and training seriously and put in place arrangements for ensuring new entrants to the profession are trained and that practitioners keep abreast of developments or extend their range of skills. The attainment of some skill level may be a condition of entry to the profession at all or be offered by the professional body for certification and authentication* of practitioners; the diploma offers reassurance to clients that the practitioners have at least some level of competence. Quality is in other words defined by the status of the provider. The desirability of certification of market research practitioners has been the subject of recent debate in the US (see Rittenburg and Murdock, 1994) and has in effect been introduced to the UK through recent changes in membership categories of the Market Research Society.

Of necessity, therefore, professions define a corpus of basic knowledge which members should have. The market research profession has such arrangements in place to achieve this and I will describe these shortly. However, there are two more general points to be made about the nature of knowledge within research. First, the intellectual roots of market research are diverse and include most of the social sciences plus statistical and other techniques borrowed from the natural as well as the social sciences. These specialisms can be deployed practically in market research with only a limited additional knowledge of the practices and techniques which are peculiar to market research. As a consequence, insistence on studying market research in any depth as a specific subject may deter entrants from other fields who can make a substantial contribution on the basis of knowledge from outside the profession. Formalisation of entry qualifications (at least to full membership) by the MRS may for this reason be counterproductive. In any case, the research profession until now has been very open and barriers to membership, rather than raising standards and skills, may reduce its inclusivity and status through leaving some credible practitioners on the outside.

The second general point about market research knowledge is that however deep it may be, it tends to be underrated by the business world in general and clients in particular. This point can be illustrated in relation to questionnaire design. Getting a questionnaire right and ensuring it is an effective tool is not an easy matter and calls for considerable skill and expertise. But because it is 'just questions' and questions are intrinsic to ordinary life, everybody is an expert or thinks that they are (see O'Brien, 1987). In other areas too, market research is not seen as offering much over and above 'common sense' or the sort of general abilities expected from university graduates. This is not the situation in other professional business services; eg lay clients will not normally argue with their accountant about how financial statements should be put together. This situation inevitably affects the general standing of researchers (and

---

* Certification implies a project to encourage all practitioners to hold the certificate, while authentication is less ambitious, implying that the certificate implies the practitioner is competent but does not rule out adequate skills being found in the non-tested. The difference in practice is based on the power of the profession to define 'true' professionals.

consequently their economic rewards) but arguably it sometimes gets in the way of quality; researchers are not always trusted to use techniques that, while effective, are not easily understood. Also the researcher's diagnosis of client needs may not be believed and instead work is geared to only superficial wants.

PROFESSIONAL ORGANISATION

Professions are invariably organised as formal bodies with constitutions, codes, management, services to members and the public and may own substantial assets. In the UK the grander bodies have Royal Charters. However, organisation and structure alone does not define professions and some bodies neither have nor claim such a status. Some professions have a number of more or less competing bodies but in the UK there is only one substantial body covering the market research profession – the MRS – and no other organisation disputes the MRS's claim to pre-eminence.* At the time of writing the MRS is celebrating its golden jubilee and since 1946 has grown from 23 enthusiasts for a new-fangled but as then unregarded business tool, to an organisation of some 7500 members with a full-time staff and an extensive range of services. The aims of the Society are formally stated as:

- To ensure that professional standards are maintained in all types of market, social and economic research.
- To promote the UK market research profession and highlight its contribution to the business community and society.
- To provide an educational, information and social platform for members.

The first aim at least clearly has some links to quality.

The organisational structure of the Society is defined by a constitution with major policies decided by members and implemented by an elected Council (whose members often overlap with other market research bodies) and salaried staff headed by a Director General.

With its members drawn from the full breadth of market research, there is a need for subgroupings (interest groups) bringing together a specialist field of interest, eg Business and Industrial Group (a sort of successor to IMRA); GIMRA, concerned with researching the general insurance market; and Census for members with a bent to demographics. There are

---

* The Industrial Marketing Research Association used to be a partial competitor although only for practitioners working in the area suggested by the title, but this body collapsed some years ago.

also some specialist professional interest bodies formally outside the Society such as the Association of Qualitative Research Practitioners, although most members of this and some other bodies are likely to be also in the MRS.

A major strand in maintaining standards is the education and training activities of the MRS. The Society, alone or in conjunction with other bodies, offers formal professional qualifications; three gradings of knowledge based certification – Foundation, Certificate and Diploma – and a parallel range of competence based National Vocational Qualifications (which as yet has had little uptake). Society membership grading is now linked to the attainment of either knowledge or competence based levels (although existing members escaped these rigours) and this may provide an impetus for future uptake. To date membership of an 'open' Society has indicated interest and perhaps commitment without any guarantee of professional competence. Undoubtedly, the knowledge and skills of members are quite variable although in various ways the Society at least defines commonly acceptable minimum standards of competence. Whether the new emphasis on certification will truly raise standards or simply ensure that many doing research stay out of the MRS, remains to be seen.

Specific programmes are in place to assist candidates attain the qualifications offered by the Society and there are numerous short courses and seminars held (very largely relying on unpaid tuition from senior members) to provide training in specific techniques and skills and to keep members up to date. The MRS also acts as a learned society by providing a forum for disseminating advances in knowledge. This includes publishing the *Journal of the Market Research Society*, the *Proceedings* of the annual conference (which is also of course a major social event) and the output of special working parties. As well as communication, these forums also serve as an arena for debate and peer group review which provides some validation for new techniques.

As in other professions and fields, no single practitioner is likely to absorb even a substantial part of this output and at best will confine his or her interest to a specialist field. Much of the content of the publications and other forums is tentative rather than definitive and this is an inevitable aspect of it being leading-edge. Also it perhaps reflects the uncertain basis of true knowledge in social sciences. Some of the subjects covered are also remote from the day-to-day interests of practitioners whose primary interest is to make a living and the proportion of the membership involved in this sort of advancement of knowledge is quite small (as no doubt it is in other professions). However, some of the discussion and the real quality improvements implied, trickle down in diffuse ways to practitioners too busy or unwilling to put the effort into direct study. The publications also provide a corpus of knowledge which any researcher can consult as the need arises.

Another role of the MRS is as a public relations and pressure group to promote the interests and value of market research. This activity overlaps with the interests of research suppliers and buyers and can lead to conflicts between the professional and commercial faces of market research. However, since the managers of at least the supply side of commercial research are in nearly all cases members of the Society and some sit on both sets of governing bodies, any dissension is usually resolved without major upset.

CODES AND STANDARDS

One aspect of professional bodies in general and the MRS in particular, which I have not yet considered, is the role of codes of practice and the extent to which these differ from quality standards. These have important consequences for quality.

Professional bodies usually have formal codes of conduct or practice and the MRS is no exception. Such codes may be referred to as professional standards but there is a difference between codes of practice and standards which I will discuss shortly. Codes are also different to the constitutions of the professional bodies. Any organisation needs a constitution of some sort to define such as who can join, how decisions will be made for the organisation, who will take them etc. Constitutions therefore regulate the organisation. Codes of practice and conduct, by contrast, regulate members – they are expected to agree to the code (as a condition of membership), more or less know its contents and, as far as is required, to put its requirements into practice in their professional work.

Codes typically relate to how members of a professional body should conduct themselves in their relations with each other, with their clients and with the wider world. They may also define some general principles about the nature of professional work and its boundaries; in effect what activities fall outside professional services – these may be forbidden to members or it may be enough for members to make clear to clients etc where the boundaries lie. Codes may, therefore, include principles which will affect how work is carried out and, therefore, they define quality in some way. Codes may go further and in some detail define how work or specific aspects of it should be carried out, but in such cases codes are incorporating some element of standards.

The Code of Conduct of the MRS (MRS, 1996) runs to some 14 pages. It is amended and revised from time to time and an up-to-date version is included in the Society's Year Book (it is also separately printed).

65

Helpfully, a one-page summary of key principles precedes the full code and this is reproduced as Figure 4.1.

A substantial part of the MRS code relates to responsibilities to informants; people who are interviewed or otherwise contribute to primary market research. Market research is based on confidential responses which are used for research purposes only and not for such as follow-on sales contact. Normally, this means that individual responses are aggregated before being passed to the client and are not identifiable as relating to a particular respondent. In most cases there is in fact little point in reporting responses on an individual basis since those interviewed are only representative of some wider population which is the subject of interest and the point of collecting data from them is to provide a basis for generalisation. The Code's requirements in relation to respondent confidentiality have, in some circumstances, legal force through the Data Protection Act (to which the Code specifically refers).

There are, however, some types of research where the responses from specific individuals (or organisations) can be an important part of the findings and conclusions. Business to business research often falls into this category since most business or industrial markets are highly skewed with a very few players accounting for a high proportion of output and consumption. For example, a survey of telecommunication providers which omitted British Telecom would be seriously biased. This aspect of the markets being studied must obviously be taken into account by the research designer in drawing the interview sample and individual responses also need to be considered when preparing findings and drawing conclusions. Provided the responses are just seen by the researcher, no problem with the principle of respondent confidentiality arises. However, clients also often want to know the position amongst a handful of market leaders on an individual basis and for legitimate reasons; a meaningful interpretation of the findings may require this. Occasionally, in such cases, the researcher may face a real dilemma in abiding by the Code and meeting the needs of the client. The problem may in some cases, but not all, be resolved if the respondent has given permission for passing on his or her individual responses.*

The respondent confidentiality requirement of the code is not just a matter of protecting respondents but also differentiating 'true' market research from other activities (covered in the part of the Code relating to the general public and business community). Such as telemarketing,

---

* The Code allows for individual responses to be passed on to clients providing the respondent gave his or her express permission for this to be done at the time of interview. It is also acceptable to report the names of organisations included in a survey but not normally the names of individual respondents or the responses attributable to specific organisations.

Key principles

The key principles of professional market research have been taken from the full text of the Code of Conduct drawn up by the Market Research Society and is binding on its members. These summarised key principles cannot be taken as a substitute for the full Code of Conduct, which is binding on members, as is the Data Protection Act.

Responsibilities to informants

- Informant's identity must not be revealed without their consent to anyone not directly involved in the research, or used for any other than research purposes. (Code Reference A2)

- Nobody shall be adversely affected or embarrassed as a direct result of participating in a research study. (Code Reference A7)

- Interviewers must always show proof of identity to informants, giving the name, address and phone number of the research agency conducting the study. (Code Reference A9/10)

- Informants must not be coerced or subjected to unwelcome intrusion and must have the rights both to respected privacy and to withdraw their co-operation at any time. (Code Reference A19/20)

- No child under 14 shall be interviewed without parent's/guardian's/responsible adult's consent, nor any young person aged 14–17, if the subject of the interview is sensitive. (Code Reference A19/20)

Responsibilities to the general public and business community

- Other activities (eg, selling, opinion moulding and collection of personal data) shall not under any circumstance be misrepresented as market research. (Code Reference B2)

- Market research shall be honest and objective and neither research methods nor findings may be used to mislead. (Code Reference B3)

Responsibilities to clients

- Client's identity, information about their business, and their commissioned market research data and findings shall remain confidential to the clients unless both client and agency agree details of any publications. (Code C5/15/17/17)

- Full methodological details of each project undertaken must be supplied to the client. (Code Reference C10)

General

- All written or verbal assurances made by anyone involved with or commissioning or conducting a study must be factually correct and honoured.

- Everyone subject to the Code of Conduct must adhere to its full provisions, protect and enhance the ethical and professional reputation of market research and ensure, whenever possible, that all others connected with studies are aware of, and abide by, the provisions of the Full Code.

Figure 4.1 *MRS Code of Conduct*

face-to-face selling and marketing database building are recognised as legitimate activities in their own right but, in the view of the Society, should be carried out in such a way that their purpose is clear and not disguised as market research; selling in the guise of market research ('sugging') is considered illegitimate, intrinsically dishonest and an activity which lessens public acceptance of market research. The building of marketing databases, which is very much a growth phenomenon, however, has presented new problems for differentiating market research from other marketing tasks. These difficulties have commercial roots in that some research agencies are increasingly involved in this type of work while on the other hand database providers outside the market research industry have started to compete with 'true' research agencies in the provision of such as market profile data. The MRS has recently included guidelines on this subject as supplement to the Code but further changes and developments are likely in this area.

In relation to clients, the Code generally avoids impinging on commercial considerations and the nature of the contract between research supplier and client, although the use of subcontractors in research has to be revealed to the client (in recognition that who is doing the work is an important matter). Mirroring respondent confidentiality, however, are requirements for keeping information about or supplied by the client confidential and this includes keeping even the identity of the client confidential (eg from respondents); the fact that a particular company has an interest at all in a market or product may be commercially sensitive. For various practical reasons, quite apart from the client's interest, research agencies may prefer, in any case, not to identify clients.

The Code, in relation to clients, also contains elements which are in effect standards and which lay down in some detail how some aspects of the work should be carried out. In particular, there is a requirement for full methodological details of research to be provided to clients. This is in recognition that the validity and 'weight' of research findings can only be evaluated if how the data were obtained is known in some detail. The requirements in this respect specified in the Code are, therefore, a standard for the presentation of research findings and as such are concerned with the quality of work. There are also fairly detailed requirements for the retention of records from research (eg the original questionnaires) and again these constitute a standard affecting the quality of work and service.

The above comments highlight some aspects of the code which are relevant to the subject of this book but readers should not take it as even a summary of the Code (the statement of key principles as reproduced is accompanied by a warning about the need to consult the full Code). As with any such code, however, merely having it in place is no guarantee

that practitioners will abide by it. The MRS has procedures for enforcement of its Code up to quasi judicial hearings which can lead to the expul-
sion of erring members. However, it is fair to say that only the most flagrant
breaches of the Code are investigated and there is no positive method in
place to establish levels of compliance. In so far, therefore, that the Code
impinges on quality of research, it is not a very effective vehicle for giving
clients assurance about quality levels and, to be fair, this is not a primary
purpose of the Code.

A further limitation of the Code relates to knowledge of its provisions.
Whether or not it is enforced forcibly, the MRS Code, like any other code,
can only be effective if practitioners and members are aware of its provisions. I know of no research conducted to establish the situation in this
respect but from purely personal experience and anecdotal evidence I
doubt that more than a small proportion of MRS members are aware of
the more detailed provisions of the Code, eg the reporting requirements.

PROFESSIONS AND STANDARDS

As discussed above, professional codes of conduct are not, as such, statements of standards, although particular codes may well include elements
which are in effect standards. There is no reason of course why a professional body should not develop formal standards which specify in
some detail the contents of the service or professional 'product' and, therefore, in effect define key aspects of quality. Rather than develop such
standards within its professional body, the market research industry
has chosen to build them in other ways which will be discussed in later
chapters. However, it is useful to consider briefly the development of standards in a different profession; accountancy.

Up to 20 years ago, how accounts should be prepared and presented
was largely guided by only the general principle that they should provide
a true and fair view of a business situation. How this general principle
should be applied in a particular case and in a particular business was
very largely a matter for the professional judgement of an individual
accountant, although this is not to say that some approaches would be
regarded as unacceptable by any yardstick. Inevitably, however, this led
to marked variation in the basis of accounting statements and to problems of comparability between companies. Serious issues arose in particular from takeovers, where the acquirer discovered that the interpretation
of true and fair applied by the acquired company was rather different to
that used by the acquirer. Faced with pressure from both outside and
inside the profession and with some possibility of legislation being
imposed, it was agreed that the profession, through its various bodies,

should develop full and detailed standards of financial reporting. This decision was, however, not without its critics within the profession who considered that their professional integrity and skills would be compromised by having to work to a standard which might not always fit the needs of particular businesses. The work in preparing standards was considerable and was guided by both the 'best' professional opinion and a search for 'true' principles to incorporate. Inevitably, however, there were elements of compromise and arbitrariness in reaching final drafts of the standards.

Today, a comprehensive range of financial reporting standards is in place. They are issued and revised by a body set up for the purpose – The Accounting Standards Board – which has replaced earlier arrangements. These standards are compulsory within the profession and to all intents and purposes must be complied with to meet the Companies Acts. Arguably, the effect of this move to standards within this profession has been to raise the quality of financial reports to the benefit of the business community at large. However, the standards intentionally constrain how professionals (accountants) will work for their clients and undoubtedly there are many cases where the latter's 'wants' if not 'needs' are not met by adherence to the standards. Formerly, for example, the profits of a business could be improved by taking certain expenditure as 'extraordinary', with considerable latitude as to what fell within this heading. The standards, however, considerably reduce this freedom and possibly, in some cases, the effect is to give a less 'true and fair' view of a business than would have been the case under the previous lax regime.

An important point about accountancy standards is that they specify the nature of outputs produced and lay down minimum quality levels for these. Within the market research industry there are some parallels but only to a limited degree. The standards which have been developed as part of the Code of Conduct, by IQCS and more recently by MRQSA (see Chapters 8 and 9) contain some output requirements but, in general, are far more concerned with how the work should be organised and managed than with what is produced. There are various reasons for this and not least of which is a lack of consensus about what constitutes a 'good' output. This relates to the problems of 'truth' as discussed in the previous chapter.

PROFESSIONALS AND THEIR CLIENTS

The discussion of professions so far in this chapter has been very much focused on the professionals themselves. However, a justification for professional organisation and status is to safeguard the interests of clients. The basis of this is an assumption that the professional has some privileged and expert skills and knowledge to which clients – the laity – do not have access. From this principle, it follows that clients often lack the skill or knowledge to recognise their own needs (rather than 'wants') in relation to the professional service and it is part of the professional role to both identify or diagnose these needs and design a service which meets these 'true' needs. Professional work, therefore, arguably always involves some element of design using this term in a broad sense (a solicitor planning the conduct of a case is carrying out 'design' work, although the term would neither be used nor recognised).

Whether or not a profession is generally successful in working this way depends on various factors. One is that the relationship between the professional and client, and the context in which this takes place, facilitates the identification of 'true' needs. As a minimum, this implies an ongoing link and opportunities for the professional to be fully aware of the client's situation. In much *ad hoc* market research this is not the case; the practitioner has very limited opportunity to diagnose needs and instead largely responds to a brief prepared by a non-expert client* and in many cases this is sufficient because the needs are transparent and easily identified by the non-professional client. Equally, however, this can produce research of limited or negative value and possibly without the problem being even recognised.

A second factor which affects the success of the professional–client relationship is the status and standing of the professional. If the client does not believe the professional to be an expert who can provide valuable skills and knowledge which only professional training can give, then the practitioner is unlikely to be trusted to identify true needs. To a considerable extent this problem exists in market research. Often market research does not look too difficult and appears to be largely based on common sense and the general skills which can be expected in business. Partly this may be a result of the market researcher's own presentational skills making the work done transparent and, therefore, seem relatively easy. In giving real service, therefore, researchers themselves can diminish the standing of the profession.

As discussed above, professional service is characterised by a focus on needs rather than just wants. However, this itself can lead to problems and conflicts. What happens if the client insists on some wants being met which in the judgement of the professional do not correspond to true needs? Codes of conduct and other elements of professional ethics may limit the grossest mismatch in this respect by forbidding the satisfaction

---

* Of course *ad hoc* research is also commissioned by professionals who may well have successfully diagnosed their organisation's needs before an agency becomes involved.

of some sorts of wants, eg supporting a claim by spurious research results. However, often it is a matter of commercial decision how far the practitioner will satisfy less than adequate requirements. In the real world, professionals will often deliver less than a quality solution in order to meet expressed requirements, if only on the principle that if they do walk away from the project others may not.

Finally, in relation to professionals and clients, it should be noted that some would argue that professions exist to tell clients what they both want and shall be allowed to have and that, despite all the fine sentiments, professions are in fact conspiracies to serve the interests of practitioners rather than clients. One does not have to take on board the strong expression of this position (eg Illich, 1977) to recognise that professions can be self-serving and that whatever the intentions, some of the practices in place are more in the interests of members than their clients. The extent to which professions, left to themselves, can have this effect is very much linked to the extent to which they are closed rather than open and can approach a monopoly position. Market research comes no way near either condition and has little opportunity (quite apart from any intent) to be unresponsive to clients.

IS PROFESSIONALISM ENOUGH?

Market research, by most criteria, is a profession even if the wider world does not always recognise it to be one. It has a well-established professional body and high level of intellectual content. Within the profession there is some consensus about good practice and, therefore, on what makes for quality, or at least quality as excellence. This consensus is also enough to provide a body of knowledge which it is agreed should be acquired by new entrants. However, there is far from unanimity (on good practice) not only in relation to specifics and details but even the basis by which the 'good' can be determined. Furthermore the ability of the profession to ensure that quality, whatever its make-up, is delivered in practice is limited for structural reasons. Market research is very much an open profession and not all practitioners are within the professional body (and nor is it reasonable to assume that those outside are necessarily inferior in skills). Even full membership of the MRS does not guarantee any particular level of competence or ability to deliver quality (in future this might change). There is also the problem that the level of control exercised by the Code of Conduct and its enforcement is quite limited. Similarly research services are mainly delivered by research companies who are not as such members of the professional body and over which the MRS has no direct control.

Even in relation to quality as excellence, therefore, professionalism in market research has a limited ability to give assurance to the buyers and users about the quality of its output. It may be that choosing the practitioner is the most important consideration of all in seeking quality, but the institutions within market research are of only limited help in this respect. Other approaches, however, support and supplement the professional basis of quality and are discussed in later chapters. There is also the other concept of quality to consider; relative quality or satisfying clients' requirements. In this area professionalism has some implications but other approaches have more potential impact. The achievement of this kind of quality is covered in some detail in the next chapter.

5

Quality and business process

The last chapter discussed how market research is organised to provide quality on an individual, professional basis with a bias towards quality as excellence based on true and valid research. However, research is not for the most part carried out by individual, sole practitioners but by businesses – market research agencies – and the people, professional and non-professional, who make up these companies. Quality in market research is, therefore, largely delivered through a business process and understanding what this involves is the subject of this chapter.

SATISFYING CLIENTS

That market research agencies, or any businesses, must over some period satisfy clients or customers is almost a truism. No client is bound forever to any agency and, if seriously dissatisfied, the client will sooner or later take the business elsewhere. If the agency concerned consistently repeats this poor performance it will soon be out of business. Like any other business, therefore, relative quality – satisfying clients – has to be a major objective whether or not it is set out in such as a 'quality policy'.

However, the other sense of quality – quality as excellence – cannot be ignored either; some balance needs to be kept between the two types of quality. A sole pursuit of relative quality with a primary focus on client wants to the possible neglect of their needs will in the longer run be self-defeating; research output can only seem as opposed to be useful for so long. In other words, if there is a gross mismatch between satisfying wants (relative quality) and needs (quality as excellence), sooner or later the deficiencies will become apparent and the client will recognise that what was really wanted was an underlying need for 'true' research. On the other hand, a pursuit of excellence, irrespective of client wants, has its own problems. For one thing, if the satisfaction of manifest wants is ignored there is a good chance that business will not be placed; the proposal will simply be lost if it inadequately addresses stated wants even though the research proposed may be objectively the perfect solution. Also – and many research suppliers have taken a long time to realise this – clients' wants go beyond areas that correspond to any objective research needs. Confidence in the people involved in the research work and whoever sells it in, clarity in all forms of communication relating to the work, high 'quality' reporting etc are all likely to be client wants to be satisfied. Commercially, it is such considerations which often decide who shall have the research business. Finally, wants must be balanced with needs within a budget; the cost of 'best' research may be unrealistically high in relation to the client's available budget or in relation to the value of the information provided.* It may not even be possible to meet the client's needs at all within the budget proposed; the affordable research methodology may be just grossly inadequate. In most cases, however, some compromise, some trade off (see Chapman, 1988) can resolve the dilemma.

Successful commercial market research is, therefore, in these and other ways, a matter of balancing the two senses of quality and I would suggest there are four linked tasks to address in pursuit of quality in market research: the identification of client wants; deciding the extent to which these wants can be met through 'true' research; the use of effective rhetoric to persuade that the satisfaction of such wants involve meeting these needs; and finally, delivering the service in a way which enhances satisfaction over and above meeting 'objective' needs – other 'non-objective' wants are met as well.

Identification of wants and needs, of requirements, clearly has a very important place in providing a quality market research service. This is hardly any surprise given that one of the major functions of market research is to identify wants and needs of consumers and potential customers for a product or service. As a business activity, market research needs to take its own medicine and identify the wants and needs – the requirements – of its own clients. This process is at two levels. First there is a strategic need to identify general classes of wants and needs that the agency will be able to satisfy effectively, bearing in mind the resources available now or in the future. This part of the process may lead an agency

---

* As an extreme example, there is clearly no point in spending more on research than the sums which will be incurred in any related investment decision.

to seek certain types of research work eg qualitative rather than quantitative, *ad hoc* rather than continuous etc, or specialise in a market sector. There is also the linked question of how the agency will be able to develop some form of competitive advantage in satisfying these identified requirements. What will, or does, make the agency special? As much as being part of need identification, these areas are the core of business planning.

The second level of identification of requirements is at the particular level; in relation to an individual client. In *ad hoc* research this translates to 'taking a brief' from a client; understanding the background to and need for the research, identifying other requirements etc. Whether classed as wants or needs, these requirements will also include some element of the budget and timetable available.

Whether at the strategic or specific level, assumptions are usually made (they may even be researched!) about clients' general requirements irrespective of the particular project. What turns the client on? Possible categories include 'true' research, the ability to meet promises and objectives, creativity, professional working methods, honouring of contract terms, timeliness, clarity in communication, adding value to 'mere' facts and many other things. Some of these – those which the generality of buyers want and suppliers are willing to provide – can be incorporated into industry-wide standards: more of this later.

As set out above, identification of requirements in market research all sounds rather impersonal and bloodless. In practice, however, identifying requirements at the particular level has a very strong personal element. For one thing it involves individual skills to have the necessary rapport with clients fully to understand the requirements. In addition, however, the process of identification of requirements, paradoxically, also delivers some of them. A universal client requirement is to have confidence in the service and output provided by the agency. Without that confidence the results cannot be used to guide decisions; the whole point of buying research. There are various ways in which an agency can offer that confidence; past performance, reputation and image in the market, independent quality assurance (to be discussed in later chapters) are all important, but nearly always confidence is bound up with individuals. The ability of the agency to deliver depends on faith and trust in Peter Jackson or whoever fronts the service (see also Callingham and Smith, 1994).

As an industry, market research has long recognised the need for personal skills to be used to build confidence in the ability to identify and deliver client requirements. However, there are also some business problems entailed in this. In a very small agency, a service based on the qualities of the particular individual is realistic but less so as you move up the size scale to where a larger team will be inevitably involved. The individual taking a brief may well not even write the proposal, let

77

alone manage the project, and by far the large majority of research is in practice carried out by operations well above the level where one individual largely determines the quality of output. In these situations confidence needs to be based on something more than personal chemistry even if buyers do not always recognise this. And on the supplier side, a predominant emphasis on the personal also has its problems – the business becomes over-dependent on the reputation of individuals and this can seriously inhibit growth. There is a limit to the number of clients the 'star' can even contact, let alone handle. The problems of confidence building and how it is achieved, whether by an emphasis on the personal or otherwise, has a close link with the identification of requirements, but it is also a much wider issue to which I shall return.

CONFORMITY TO SPECIFICATION

Once and however identified, client requirements including general 'turn-ons', at the individual project level, can be set out as part of a specification. This will also include some statement of the outputs which will be delivered to meet these requirements. The most common tangible form of such a specification is a research proposal (at least it is in *ad hoc* research). However, the 'full' specification of what is required and will be delivered is always greater than what is normally covered in a proposal document. For one thing there may be an implicit assumption of professional standards of practice beyond what is formally set down and this may include that any methods used will conform to generally recognised and valid practice. There are also the requirements that relate to service outside the area of objective research practice – good communication, clarity in reporting, timeliness, levels of client contact and involvement. Some of these may be covered explicitly in a proposal while others may be set out in promotional literature or standard operating procedures or as part of a formal quality policy. An agreed and recognised industry standard may also apply.

However set out, and even if part of it is implicit, a specification for the research project will exist and should be recognised by the supplier and, as far as practical, explicitly agreed with the client. Difficulties arise and serious quality problems result where this specification leaves out some important requirements, since unaware of what is required, there is no possibility that the supplier can anywhere near satisfy the client. If, however, a more or less complete specification is achieved, quality becomes a matter of meeting that specification; meet it in all important particulars and quality is achieved, fail to do so in one or more areas and the service provided is less than high quality. Here then is another sense of quality – conformity to specification.

Day to day, conformity to specification is an effective way of opera-
tionalising quality in a business process and will be a theme throughout
the rest of this book. This sense of quality, it should be noted, bridges
both relative quality and quality as excellence since both should be
balanced in the specification. However, achieving quality through conformity to specification does require a thorough understanding of requirements and a full specification. It is emphatically not just a matter of
technically 'good' research with a disregard for the less objective client
requirements which may also need articulating formally, whether as part
of a research proposal or as general statements about what an agency
delivers to its clients. The specification also needs to be fully understood
throughout the team involved and this cannot just be left to chance.

Although this pre-empts some later comments, it is worth noting here
that the concept of conformity to specification can be criticised for its
static nature. Client requirements change and are changed by suppliers,
and specifications once set may miss this point. There is also the issue of
whether the aim should be mere satisfaction rather than something more;
delighting for example. However, more of this later.

QUALITY AND MONEY

The issue of money has already been mentioned in the context of clients'
wants and needs, but money also has another dimension in quality.
Research organisations are private sector undertakings which are bound
to have commercial objectives of some sort. In effect they need to attain
an adequate level of performance on one or more financial performance
measures. These may include profit, cashflow, shareholder value and net
worth or just the income of the principals (in at least smaller agencies,
making a 'good' living may be considered a quite adequate financial
performance). What is adequate will depend on various circumstances and
quite often performance is well below any optimum – market research
companies tend to be 'uncommercial' in this sense. However, financial
performance cannot be ignored or ignored indefinitely and, therefore, has
to be considered in relation to quality.

Bringing money into quality is usually by some caveat of 'least cost'.
Customer requirements will be met at least cost, or conformity to specification will be at least cost. Least cost is regarded as the mirror of most
profit although this congruence is not strictly speaking logically watertight.
In one sense, least cost can compromise what is delivered to the customer;
frozen peas may be least cost, but for a certain quality of meal I will be
less than satisfied if these are served instead of fresh mangetout. Similarly
a quota sample of 500 may be cheaper than a random walk of 1000
but may be inadequate to meet the purpose to which the research is

being put. However, least cost is a valid concept if considered post-specification. Once what will be delivered is defined and agreed, least cost becomes a matter of efficiency.

Efficiency as an aspect of market research tends to be unregarded; at least in the literature – there is an enormous wealth on what should be delivered in terms of true research but surprisingly little on how research can be conducted efficiently and I do not think that this is just a matter of such a commercial consideration being unsuitable for the professional press. At least in some areas, research has been a fortunate trade with high enough margins to make efficiency a not obviously pressing matter. Also many agencies are not business performance optimisers. However, this may change and has changed in the more commercially oriented companies big and small. There are three main areas to seek efficiency in market research; in methods of working, in productivity and in minimisation of errors.

Methods of working include internal organisation. The classic means to efficiency in the industrial age was division of labour – Adam Smith's pin works and all that. In market research the level of division of labour is largely a function of agency size; only at certain levels of output can staff be dedicated to a narrow range of tasks. Working against division of labour is, however, the need for flexibility to deliver the service. Dedicated staff need to be brought into other tasks if the need is there. Division of labour also stands in the way of communication and, often therefore, service delivery; the field manager is not in contact with the client directly and the research executive has little grasp of the practicalities of getting the work into the field. Similarly, poor communication reduces understanding of the specification to be met and thus the chances of delivering quality. Of course these problems can be overcome in various ways. One way is to have an effective quality system, although the need for this can be regarded as a consequence of the division of labour. Another approach is a team focus – again, the need for this is also partly a result of the division of labour.

It may appear from the above that I am suggesting that various forms of non-specialist flexibility are always better than a pronounced division of labour in market research, but this is not my intention. Division of labour is always a means to be considered in the pursuit of efficiency providing that any problems it creates do not outweigh the realisable benefits. Most agencies have paradoxically both too much and too little division of labour, with tasks that need to be integrated divided and tasks that would be better divided, integrated.

The question of getting the balance right in relation to division of labour is of course not the only aspect of working methods which affect efficiency. Others include the degree of pyramid versus flat-structure organisation, the effectiveness of team working over and above as a cure for the communication problems arising from the division of labour and the whole issue of skills building. All these can aid efficiency and, therefore, deliver quality at least cost. However, there is another aspect of efficient working methods, critical in manufacturing industry, but which has only more recently come to the fore in market research; capital investment. In market research, as increasingly elsewhere, capital investment now largely resolves itself as information technology (IT).

IT has made considerable inroads in market research already and the process of computerisation will continue both vertically (reaching into all sizes of operations) and horizontally (involving more functions and processes). The initial wave of IT was in data processing and at first through analysis packages (I can remember when at least small volume work was largely hand analysed) and more recently through mechanised data entry systems (see Rust and Cooil, 1994; Klose and Ball, 1995). Next IT came to dominate reporting and client communication; word processing, computer graphics and computerised presentations. Now IT is becoming central to data collection with computer aided interviewing used more and more in both phone (CATI) and face to face (CAPI) based research. The efficiency of this is a function of both improvements offered in questionnaire administration and the cutting out or reduction of separate data entry. On the horizon may be speech recognition systems which will take the process still further (see Blyth and Piper, 1994). These and other facets of IT have had a major impact on efficiency and, therefore, the potential to deliver quality research at least cost. Two other aspects of this process to be noted are a certain bias towards larger companies since it is they who can more readily afford the investment level involved, and that IT itself has an impact on other aspects of quality.

Addressing or monitoring individual productivity appears to have been even less of an issue in research than efficiency more generally. This is strange in that labour costs in market research predominate and one way or another any attempt to improve efficiency must consider the question of labour productivity. One problem in the way is the difficulty of measuring output which is essential to any serious attempt to define and improve productivity. In the long run, project norms can be established for data collection and data processing productivity per operator but this is much harder in short-run *ad hoc* work; by the stage at which output norms can be defined, the work is half finished.

Even more problematical is the issue of research executive or professional productivity; how much time should be devoted to a questionnaire, a proposal or report? One executive may produce a 'standard' proposal in half a day and another might take a whole day over the same job; so is the first more efficient? Only if he or she wins the business. A half day spent on a lost proposal is inefficient by any measure. What I am alluding to is that seeming productivity may be at the expense of quality – of meeting the specification – but that the differences may be very difficult to measure or even recognise. The lost proposal is clearcut; the problems of the hastily drafted questionnaire or report may not be so transparent. In any sort of non-routine work, and much of market research falls into this category, there is likely to be some trade-off between time spent and quality of output, although the law of diminishing returns also applies.

The last aspect of efficiency to consider is error reduction, or more precisely errors identified in the research process. In manufacturing industry, errors or defects in the process result in rejects and scrap and the benefits of a quality approach are very often discussed in the context of reducing these levels – do it right and do it right first time. Research output is, however, seldom scrapped in the manufacturing sense and instead identified errors are more likely to be reworked; the document is redrafted, the booked interviewers are put on hold, poor interviews are repeated, oversight in the analysis specification leads to repunching and extra runs etc. So even though there is little in the way of visible scrap levels, there is nearly always potential to tighten up on process error in research and so reduce costs.

Even more important, error reduction improves quality in the sense of matching requirements. This may be through avoiding delays and so meeting timing requirements but also because some level of detected error is in practice often not reworked; the error is not 'big enough'. Also some sorts of error are difficult to identify at all or it is a matter of judgement whether it is an error. Is an uninspired report an error? Finally it should be recognised that in market research (and other services) error reduction in the process has a special importance because many just cannot be detected in the final report. Bad data collection does not look any different to good when the results are set out in the report.

This brings me to the more general point that changes introduced to improve efficiency in the process may do more for quality than achieve it at least cost, since the new practices make the output better in some sense. This is very clear in relation to new technology. CATI and CAPI for example reduce or obviate errors from interviewer routeing or allow the questionnaire to be administered in a way that might be just too unwieldy by traditional methods. Similarly logic checks are now routinely built into data processing which at least identify (even if they do not always solve) errors in data collection or coding. Even something as now commonplace as a computer generated cross analysis permits a degree of error avoidance that was almost impossible to achieve with manual methods (I remember labouring for days to try and get large matrices to add up both down and across). Quality of output may also be improved by other sorts of changes primarily introduced to improve efficiency; team working may for example bring new creativity to reporting and a formal quality system should at least improve the consistency of the service provided as well as making the process more efficient.

DELIVERING MARKET RESEARCH QUALITY THROUGH THE BUSINESS PROCESS

Figure 5.1 summarises the various elements of quality I have discussed in this chapter. Conformity to specification should take account of both quality as excellence and relative quality, and quality has to be delivered within a commercial environment; at least cost.

Whatever is delivered in terms of quality can be more or less; more or less excellent, more or less meet client needs, to specification and at minimal cost. In other words quality can be treated as a variable and measured. All sorts of measures are possible (see Bendell *et al*, 1993) within the processes (eg error rates, instances of non-conformity to specification, production costs and productivity) or of the outputs (eg customer complaint levels, customer satisfaction, market performance, financial performance); some of these measures are more direct than others, which may reflect 'outside' factors independent of quality. Market research techniques can of course be themselves a quality measurement tool, with customer satisfaction surveys particularly to the fore in the last few years.

The measurement of quality is often hard to achieve in market research, but for now it can be accepted that research companies, like other businesses, should have as an important goal the optimisation of quality. The question is, how can this be achieved? There are very many approaches to quality optimisation within business with different ones emphasised or fashionable at different times and in different business areas (and more or less appropriate depending on the application). They can all, however, be reasonably summarised as within four classifications or business quality models; professional responsibility, quality control, quality assurance and total quality management (TQM). Each model is discussed below and in relation to their effectiveness within three key elements of a business which were mentioned in Chapter 1: commitment, process and people. To recap, commitment to quality from top to bottom within an organisation is always essential. Process is how the business is organised and works to deliver quality to the client and clearly nothing can be done at all without people, and particularly so in businesses such as market research. Although it is useful, analytically, to separate these three elements they clearly do not in any sense exist independently; they are all aspects or perspectives of a unity, of a business. Figure 5.2 links the business quality models with the three elements.

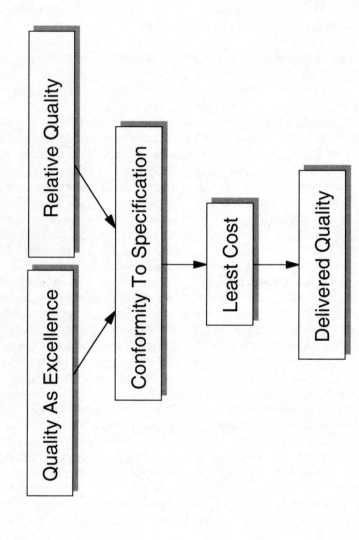

Figure 5.1 *Elements of quality*

Professionalism has been discussed at some length in the previous chapter. The issue here, however, is how effective is it as a quality model within a business rather than at the individual practitioner level? As already indicated, problems and tensions arise in any link-up of professionalism and the business process and the difficulties can be discussed within the context of the effectiveness of the professional responsibility model within the business elements of commitment, process and people. Professional responsibility is very effective in building a commitment to quality amongst members of a profession, including in market research. This is achieved through values (a commitment to excellence, truth etc), professional institutions and the way new members of the profession are inducted. All of these carry across to a commitment to quality within an organisation led by professionals, and market research agencies are invariably led by research professionals. Professional responsibility also works very well at the people level through the strong emphasis on professional education, both initial and continuing, and the advancement of professional knowledge (the MRS and other bodies in their role as learned societies).

Yet in Figure 5.2 the effectiveness of professional responsibility as a business quality model is only marked as medium for both commitment and people. Why? Within a market research business, not all or even the majority of staff are of professional status; there are also the various support staff and the ratio of these tends to be higher in the larger agencies. Even more important are the legions of interviewers working in the field or phone centres. Professional responsibility tends in practice to bypass these staff and whatever commitment to quality they may have. The professional/non-professional gulf can even emphasise the division and difference. Even 'near' professionals such as field controllers can consider themselves to be second class.

The even greater limitation of professional responsibility, however, lies in relation to process. Just because professionalism is focused at the individual level it has little relevance to how a business process should be worked. At best, the model is of the senior professional controlling the process through taking responsibility for the output, coaching juniors and supervising non-professionals. In relation to process, professional responsibility is amateur.* But until at least recently this was the implicit model for quality within market research.

The limitations of professional responsibility as a business quality model are linked to size. Its limitations in relation to process only really become apparent above a certain organisational size and division of labour. In an agency of a couple of experienced practitioners with a few helpers

---

* In my view (and this may be mere prejudice) other activities such as law, dominated by the professional ethos, commonly display an inability or indifference to managing process.

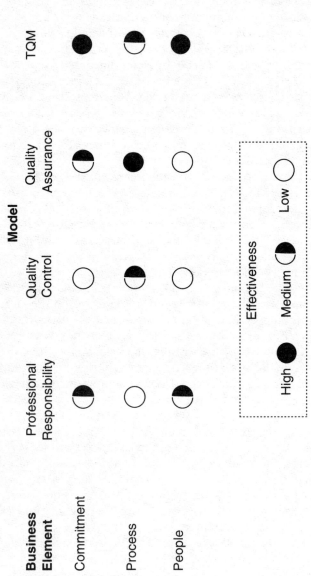

Figure 5.2 *Four business quality models*

(and many still are of this size) process problems are either less evident or can be solved in the informal manner possible within the professional responsibility model. In even medium sized agencies, however, real thought and effort have to be put into managing the processes and the increase of interest in other models may, in part, reflect the growth of agency size.

The other models for delivering quality are all rooted in manufacturing industry and have been imported and adapted to service industries such as market research. Quality control is the oldest of them and has long been the backbone of product quality within industry. At its crudest, quality control works by having a quality 'policeman' stand by the gate of the factory and inspect all (or a sample of) products awaiting shipment. The inspection will be against some template of what is required and may involve testing of physical properties or functioning. Products which match up to pre-set criteria go off to the customer while those which do not go into the scrap skip or back for reworking. Process is, therefore, controlled through the output only. This model was (and is still) widely used in manufacturing and, while it may be better than nothing, it self evidently does not address commitment or people at all, except negatively. Rejection, as the only output of quality, is hardly much of a motivator.

Quality control also has some fairly obvious limitations even in relation to process. For one thing scrap represents waste and unnecessary costs but within the model nothing is done to address why scrap arises or why the rates go up or down. The output of quality control of this sort is inefficiency and with the underlying problems not considered, no remedies can be sought or found. Also, who is to say the 'policeman' is up to the job or that the criteria by which products are judged correspond to requirements. In market research the application of the quality control model in this form is clearly of little value since the quality of research can scarcely, or only very partially, be inspected in any final output. A check of a written report may pick up typing errors, poor layout or even an inadequate coverage of the research objectives, but even if it 'passes' it still does not say the work is any good; the research design may be poor, or badly executed, the data collection haphazard or full of errors and the analysis may have made everything worse. Curtains at the window are not always a sign of respectability within.

Quality control can be made more effective in relation to process if it is brought into the workplace. In this variant, the total process is broken down and inspection carried out on the output of each critical subprocess (which is of course the input of the next subprocess). This is far more effective. At least problems are picked up earlier so that later processes are not wasted working on already defective product. Also, when errors are found, we know at which part of the process to look if we are going to find ways of solving the problems. However, even in this variant, the quality control model is negative rather than positive in outlook and there is nothing within it to help find why things go wrong or put them right. Also it still has nothing to do with commitment or skilling-up people; in fact with the 'policemen' in the factory, morale is probably worse.

However, such intermediate quality control has more of a potential role in market research than final inspection and it is, in practice, used effectively. Research designs, questionnaires and reports may be checked by more senior staff and the output from data collection, and possibly data processing, is often checked or verified in ways not unlike the methods used in manufacturing. The Interviewer Quality Control Scheme (IQCS) – note 'quality control' – prescribes such methods in data collection and the standards of the Market Research Quality Standards Association (MRQSA) do so across a wider spectrum of the market research process – both IQCS and MRQSA are discussed below and in later, dedicated chapters.

Quality assurance, the third business quality model, is often misunderstood. Either the difference between quality control is not grasped or it is assumed, wrongly, to be about the setting of product or service standards (which are, not surprisingly, then found to be wanting). The focus of quality assurance is how things are produced (or the service carried out) rather than the characteristics of what is produced; finding effective or best ways of managing the process to minimise defects and errors. A key objective of this model is the systematic investigation and solving of problems. Methods include tools such as a formal quality system, internal auditing and management involvement; quality assurance is a model for the active management of quality and, therefore, involvement. Quality assurance also builds in steps to ensure requirements are defined and met.

Inspection and testing are not in principle intrinsic to quality assurance and ideally the objective may be to obviate the necessity for much of this 'wasted' effort; solve the underlying causes of error and there will be no need for inspection and testing. In practice though, quality assurance invariably incorporates some quality control elements (with good effect) and may be introduced as a next step to a quality control sytem. However, the point may be partly missed if quality assurance is just crudely superimposed; the limitations of quality control are then not surpassed.

Quality assurance clearly aims to address process in a far-reaching way. It also involves commitment to some degree; it will certainly only work if management believe in it and believe that managing quality has a high priority. Other staff also have to work at quality and in this sense commitment to some level is needed for the approach to work. However, commitment is not engendered by quality assurance as such; it needs to be inspired from 'outside'. Quality assurance is also scarcely people orien-tated; they at best only appear as role players and then unidimensionally; as 'operators', 'investigators' or 'representatives'.

In the last few years, quality assurance has made an impact on and inroads into market research, with companies implementing ISO 9000 (a standard for quality assurance) and MRQSA, giving the concept a central place in its standards. IQCS too, implicitly if not explicitly, incor-porates quality assurance thinking. Because of its growing importance (and because I am a fairly strong believer), quality assurance is strongly featured in the remaining chapters, including Chapter 6 and Chapter 7 (which cover ISO 9000). How it can be made to work in market research is also discussed in some detail in Chapter 12.

A point to note about both quality control and quality assurance is that the specification of what should be attained in quality terms comes from outside and particularly from customers and clients; their requirements. Quality control takes this as given while quality assurance should in-corporate methods for establishing or checking what these are. However, quality assurance has no built-in standards of product or service quality. It is a method for ensuring that such standards, whatever these are, are identified and met constantly or consistently, but it is not a method of defining them. As an aid to both customers and suppliers, it may be found useful to define requirements and the specification wholly or partly in terms of some recognised and independent standard. Quality, or at least minimum quality, then becomes a matter of conformity to the standard. In manufacturing, quality standards, particularly British Standards (BSs) are very well established. As yet, however, the impact in services is very much less and in this respect market research is a leader. Both the 10-year-old IQCS minimum standards and the more recent MRQSA stan-dards fall into this category and both are the subject of separate, later chapters (Chapter 8 and Chapter 9).

Although product or service standards are not defined within quality assurance models, there is a link. Quality assurance provides a method of ensuring that output is consistently to the minimum standards. The BSI for example offers its Kitemark service to give third party assurance that a business's output is to a defined BS (or other) product standard. However, a prior condition of awarding the Kitemark is that the business has effective quality assurance in place through ISO 9000. MRQSA has adopted a similar approach (but not with a requirement for ISO 9000).

The final model of business quality to consider is Total Quality Management (TQM). This is generally seen as setting quality goals more demanding than is common with the quality assurance approach. From the TQM perspective, quality assurance is about ensuring that a given level of quality is met (ie a product standard). This is all very well, but is not, it is said, going to ensure long term competitive advantage. Instead, quality should be viewed dynamically, existing standards exceeded and the achievements of other organisations 'benchmarked'. Rather than merely satisfying the customer, the aim should be to delight; to bring him or her into a love affair with the supplier by giving 'extras' that he or she was not even aware were worth having. Quality itself, therefore, becomes a process and one with an ideal but not an attainable end. The pursuit of quality is for ever and ever. This all may sound very hyped but then that is the nature of TQM. Some critics argue that excited disciples and jargon are the more characteristic outputs than any real improvements.

Some would also contend that TQM sets up artificial limitations to quality assurance so that the new methods can claim to surpass them. Arguably, meeting requirements – fully meeting requirements – which quality assurance recognises is no different from delighting customers. Also effective quality assurance programmes recognise that customers wants and needs change and shift with time – partly because of the efforts of suppliers to give new experiences – and that quality, therefore, is not and cannot be static. However, TQM cannot simply be dismissed, if only because of its level of uptake. Also it is not necessarily a competitor of quality assurance; it can be an extension. Some approaches to TQM regard quality assurance as necessary underpinning on which further progress can be built. Others, however, are hostile; at least to quality assurance built around standards such as ISO 9000 which are said to be too rigid.

It is not easy to characterise what TQM involves in practice, since it encompasses a wide range of methods and techniques. In all versions, however, there is a very strong emphasis on people and their commitment to the process of quality improvement. Much is made of realising the potential of staff to enable them to deliver quality to their customers and clients. Staff with no access to 'real' customers are encouraged to regard other staff as internal customers. TQM is soft and fuzzy, yet is often accompanied with messianic fervour and a hearts-and-minds outlook. Empowerment, skill enhancement, team building, managers as facilitators, quality circles and open, learning organisations are all alternative or overlapping techniques within a TQM approach.

A framework around which to implement the staff development techniques within TQM is the Investor In People (IiP) standard (although this can be taken up without a conscious subscription to TQM). IiP is discussed in Chapter 10.

Process is certainly not ignored in TQM although, in some versions, planning changes to process comes out of and follows changing people; right ways come from right people. However, other approaches involve a

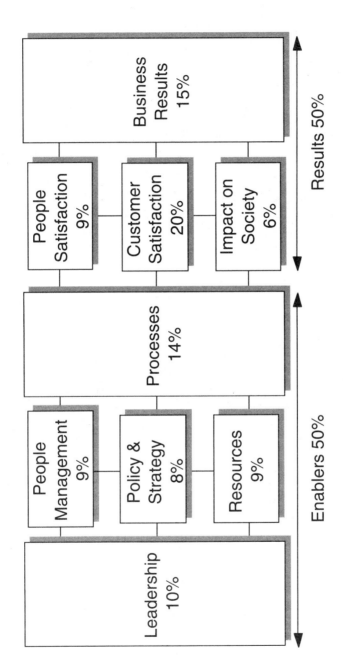

Figure 5.3 *UK/European model for TQM*

planned review and change of processes right from the start of the programme. The British Quality Foundation, for example, promotes a UK/European model for TQM which is represented graphically in Figure 5.3. The nine elements of the model are put forward as the key components of organisational excellence and are used to assess progress towards this goal through self assessment techniques and to provide a framework for improvement planning covering not only processes but also commitment (leadership) and people. All elements of quality.

Business re-engineering, involving a radical change of business processes to achieve some substantial measurable goal (eg delivery time, cost reduction, productivity etc), can also be linked to or be a variant of TQM. Obviously, process is the focus, although the need for commitment and the need for people to change the way they work are also essential in re-engineering programmes. Business re-engineering is clearly not at the cuddly end of TQM and the reality may often involve acute pain for the participants with down-sizing (firing many of the staff) and delayering (firing management staff) to the fore. These aspects may clearly work against commitment and be seen as anti-people, although they may well improve shareholder value regardless of staff morale (which is not, after all, an end of capitalist enterprise). After a short lived vogue, re-engineering is less in fashion than it was. However, business fashions are not like clothes. Particular business sectors may adopt 'radical' approaches which are regarded as outmoded elsewhere. Similarly techniques are often rediscovered and repackaged by solution vendors (such as management consultants) and reappear in new guises. It is quite possible that as business services such as market research grow in size and complexity, re-engineering of their processes may be needed or taken up.

TQM as a self-conscious movement has made little impact in market research (although this is not to say that some companies have not consciously adopted it). However, quality as an explicit concept is still quite new in market research and TQM may come to the fore as companies digest other techniques. In practice, TQM may well take the form of a linking and amalgamation of professionalism, quality assurance, the adoption of industry minimum standards such as MRQSA and IQCS together with softer, people programmes (several research companies have taken up IiP). As an industry, little effort is needed to persuade of the importance of people to achieve quality. Techniques such as empowerment, facilitating management and the learning organisation are already often in place in market research agencies and were so before the terminology was invented.

Because of its vagueness, TQM will not be explicitly discussed elsewhere in this book but most of the elements are covered one way or another.

6

Quality assurance and ISO 9000

Since 1992 (the date when the first research company was assessed to BS 5750/ISO 9000) a substantial proportion of the top 20 agencies (and some smaller ones as well) have registered as ISO 9000 suppliers. However, the impact of this standard has been far greater than its actual uptake among research agencies. Perhaps most important has been its effect as a catalyst to an ongoing debate about quality in market research and whether or not the approach implicit in the Standard is right for the industry. Also, the perceived limitations of ISO 9000 (which in my opinion were largely rooted in a failure to understand the point and purpose of the Standard) have led to a different if complementary approach; the development of minimum service standards for market research by the Market Research Quality Standards Association (MRQSA). This is discussed in Chapter 9. An understanding of what ISO 9000 is (and is not) is, therefore, essential in a book about quality in market research. In fact so important is the topic that discussion of it is spread over two chapters. This one, which covers, in general terms, quality assurance and the ISO 9000 models for it; and the next, which covers in some detail the requirements which have to be met and how an ISO 9000 system can be implemented and certificated in a market research business.

WHAT IS ISO 9000?

In the last chapter I introduced quality assurance. ISO 9000 (or BS 5750 as it was) is a widely recognised international standard for quality assurance* and a chapter on ISO 9000 can also double as a more detailed consideration of how quality assurance can be applied in market research. However, to avoid misunderstanding, I should make it clear that effective quality assurance does not have to equate to ISO 9000. There can be, and are, other effective models, and even if a quality assurance model matching this international standard is sought, this does not have to imply formal assessment and certification.

As I have just stated, ISO 9000 is a standard or model for quality assurance and, therefore, for managing quality; for ensuring that what is produced is to specification and to requirements. The approach of the model is that of a formal and documented quality system which if effectively implemented will (it is claimed) ensure quality assurance and in some sense quality. ISO 9000, however, is not a standard for any particular quality level of product or service. What quality level should be the aim has to be defined alongside the quality assurance system; this is not to be found within ISO 9000 itself. Instead the specification of service or product requirements has to be sought in appropriate external standards (in market research these may be IQCS or MRQSA) or defined by the organisation implementing ISO 9000 and to meet the requirements of its clients. Once these standards are defined, ISO 9000 should help ensure that they are met constantly and consistently and, therefore, it is referred to as a standard of capability; a capability to meet the required levels of product or service standards. The level of defined quality (in the sense of quality as excellence) does not have to be high; if the aim is to produce cheap rubbish for those who cannot afford anything else, so be it. But, with an effective ISO 9000 system, the rubbish will not drop below some defined level of nastiness (or go beyond it). Much of the debate within market research about ISO 9000, and quality in general, was a result of a failure to understand the point that ISO 9000 is a standard for capability rather than a service or product standard and the confusion still exists.

ISO 9000 is a general model for quality assurance in the sense that it can be applied to any sort of activity and any sort of business or for that matter any sort of organisation including non-commercial ones (eg local authorities, police, health bodies have all taken it up). Because the Standard is so wide in scope, it has to be adapted and 'translated' to the needs of particular industries and, to assist implementation, many industries have produced industry-specific guidance documents showing what

---

*   For the purists, it should be noted that 'ISO 9000' is a whole series of documents. There are three standards for quality assurance within this series – ISO 9001, ISO 9002 and ISO 9003 – and the differences between them and their relevance to market research are discussed shortly.

the requirements of the Standard mean in the particular context. There is such a document for the market research industry (see MRQSA, 1995). However, having said that ISO 9000 is for any application, it is not hard, on reading the Standard, to believe that the drafters were closer to engineering than business services. The further the particular industry is from engineering type operations, the more 'translation' is needed to apply it effectively. This point certainly applies to market research.

The origins of ISO 9000 can be traced back to the defence industry which has particular need to ensure that products are consistently made to specification and meet requirements. The need for effective quality assurance in defence contractors led to an appropriate capability standard being developed – Defence Standard 05–21. As the concept of formal quality assurance and quality systems became familiar outside defence, other manufacturing industries started to require evidence that their own suppliers had effective quality assurance in place and this led in 1979 to a new British Standard – BS 5750 – against which suppliers could be assessed. BS 5750 was substantially revised in 1987 and was widely taken as a model for other countries' national quality assurance standards. Eventually an international standard – the ISO 9000 series (the European equivalent being EN 29000) was produced. BSI is committed to harmonise its national standards to any relevant international ones and, therefore, in 1994, BS 5750 was revised and republished by BSI as the BS EN ISO 9000 series of standards. Apart from within BSI, ISO 9000 suffices as a designation.

Not only must ISO 9000 be translated to the specific practices of an industry but it must be implemented to meet the unique requirements of particular organisations. Because no two organisations are the same, the requirements of ISO 9000 have to be met through a quality system developed specifically for the particular company and to fit that organisation's culture and working methods. The ISO 9000 standards, therefore, are not themselves systems which can be simply taken off the shelf and followed. A company 'doing' ISO 9000 must instead put significant effort into developing its own systems to meet its own needs as well as the requirements of the standard. If desired, the company system can also incorporate requirements not covered by ISO 9000 (eg in financial processes). Once the Standard has been implemented, the organisation can be independently assessed and certified as meeting ISO 9000 and the process involved will be described later in this chapter. However, the benefits of ISO 9000 should be far greater than any kudos from the ISO 9000 certificate. An organisation may even choose to meet the Standard but not to go to the bother and expense of assessment.

THE ESSENTIALS OF ISO 9000

The requirements of the ISO 9000 standards are set out under 20 main headings* and these are covered in some detail in the next chapter. For now I shall concentrate at a more general level on the essential features of the Standard and how these relate to market research services. These features are: design; meeting requirements; controlling the work; checking; solving problems; management; and documents and records.

DESIGN

Design, as covered by ISO 9000, is work carried out as part of a specific contract with a customer who has some sort of general requirement to be met, specified perhaps in what the final product will do – a widget is needed to perform a specific function and the supplier both designs one to perform satisfactorily and then makes it in the number required. In most 'full service' market research there is clearly such a process involved; the client has an information need and objectives which the research design meets and often this design is very tailored to one client (although drawing on experience gained in comparable projects). In a sense, design in this case is part of the contract although there is a twist to this; see shortly.

In manufacturing, however, design work is often carried out independently of a contract with a specific client. Instead a product is designed and developed to meet the general needs of a market or niche and then sold from stock. In this type of situation, a supplier seeking ISO 9000 would probably exclude design work from the scope of assessment to the standard (ie be assessed to ISO 9002) although the position is not, in this respect, clearcut. Some market research companies, and especially the larger ones, also develop designs to meet the general needs of their market or niche; proprietary research products which are then offered 'off the shelf'. It is arguable whether or not these need to be covered by the design requirements of ISO 9001 but in practice research companies generally do include them in their ISO 9000 design procedures and the industry guidelines recommend this.

Businesses carrying out no design work – producing products or services to a detailed customer-supplied specification – will generally seek ISO 9002 (the standard without design). Research companies such as 'field and tab' operations with no design element can also realistically consider ISO 9002, although few seem to have done so.

---

* More accurately ISO 9001 has 20 main headings. ISO 9002 has only 19 and ISO 9003 (not relevant to market research) has 12.

The general idea of design, as per ISO 9000, is, therefore, quite relevant to market research. But difficulties start to appear when the details are examined. The requirements in this respect of the Standard (design is covered by ISO 9001 only) are, at face value, both very demanding and difficult to meet. Also, it must be said, they do not easily fit into the market research process and an awful lot of 'squeezing' is needed to align the requirements with the established practice of market research. One immediate difficulty is that in the Standard it is assumed that design follows the contract and, therefore, after customer requirements are identified and agreed. In market research, or at least *ad hoc* research, the sequence is reversed since the fundamental element of research design normally takes place before the contract;* it is set out in a proposal and before the client enters into any commitment. There is, therefore, no contract covering the fundamental design work. Market research is, therefore, unusual in that one of the most skilled parts of the service offered to clients is, in effect, provided free of charge (although the costs are obviously recouped from clients in general). This aspect of market research design work affects how the specific requirements of the Standard, in design work, can be realistically applied. For example the requirements in the Standard relating to design and development planning, organisational and technical interfaces and design inputs, implicitly assume that these are sequential and distinct activities, but in preparing a proposal for a research client these are no more than facets of the work and are carried out together and typically by one person only. Also, since the work is 'free', there is an economic limit to how much time can be spent on preparing the proposal (practically the deciding factor is the potential pay-off – the charge level and how likely it is that the job will be won).

However, despite any apparent difficulties of applying the requirements of ISO 9000 to market research design, design work is a fundamental part of the work of a research agency and there is a clear commercial premium on getting it right or as right as possible. Not only is the design work fundamental to the quality of the research output (regardless of whether quality is a matter of meeting requirements or conformity to professional excellence) but it also affects whether or not contracts are won in the first place. Proposals not only need to be good, they need to be seen to be good (through their presentational quality and rhetoric). It is, therefore, not hard to persuade research agencies that proposal work should be

---

* Questionnaire design and detailed work related to sampling do, however, normally come after an order is placed. I have always refused to draft *ad hoc* research questionnaires before commission on grounds of superstition; these jobs never seem to go ahead.

approached in a 'right' way, with explicit decisions made in aspects of proposal writing such as who, in the agency, can and should prepare them, who should check them (although depending who – how senior – drafts proposals, it may be decided that a second person checking is not appropriate), what steps should be taken to ensure that they match client requirements and that they are commercially viable. Once a need for a more or less agency-standard approach in these areas is recognised, meeting ISO 9000 requirements in this area seems less alarming and especially as the guidelines available (see MRQSA, 1995) show reasonably well how the seemingly difficult particulars of the Standard can be adapted to fit reasonable and largely well-established market research practice.

Before moving away from design and ISO 9000, there is a further aspect worth discussing which also has echoes elsewhere in applying the Standard to market research. This is the issue of creativity. ISO 9000 is criticised for either being a dead weight on creativity or to be largely beside the point because it does not address creativity. In design work, creativity is clearly essential as it is in other aspects of research; it may be what distinguishes excellent research from the merely acceptable. What can be systematised and set out in a procedure is probably not creative by definition. Inspiration is not to be anticipated.

At one level the above is true and quality assurance methods will not of themselves create the brilliant idea or set it out to best effect. Clearly, also, it would be a poor system which inhibited staff from thinking in a creative way. However, creative processes do not happen in a vacuum and nor does a creative approach necessarily translate into a developed and worked-out research design. Appropriate staff must be assigned to design work, the requirements for the design need to be explicitly recognised and the staff and departments involved in putting the design into effect should, ideally, have an input. Ensuring these and other considerations are taken into account requires some sort of planned effort and a systematic framework should ensure that the creative input is put to best effect. Creative effort is important, but it is not all that is important – a relatively trivial mistake such as missing pages in a proposal document, which is controllable by a procedural approach, can render all creativity useless. And if the chances of things going wrong in the associated 'mechanical' processes are reduced, creative staff can concentrate on being creative.

MEETING REQUIREMENTS

Of course, the whole of ISO 9000 is about systems to meet requirements but there are some specific requirements as well. One is the need to take active steps to understand what the requirements are and make sure the organisation is able and equipped to meet these – 'contract review' in the terms of the standard. There is, in addition, a need to document the requirements in some form and review that the service to be supplied is capable of meeting requirements. In *ad hoc* market research practice, the proposal document and the work lying behind it should generally ensure that these requirements are met and documented; design work in practice, therefore, very largely covers contract review. The only additional need in this area is to document any changes which are agreed with the client post-commission. Without a formal system in place this may not be done, but few would argue on its desirability from even a purely commercial point of view. If this is done, the possibility of subsequent arguments about what the project involves should be largely avoided. Incidentally, there is no specific need for an ISO 9000 system to require clients to place orders in writing if this is considered problematical or unnecessary (and it often is).

Meeting requirements is also a matter of ensuring that once a project is agreed, it is carried out as specified and, therefore, continues to meet requirements. This is very largely a matter of project management and control which is discussed shortly. There is also a need to tell the client about things that go wrong or where the output does not meet the specification. This may be a difficult matter commercially, but is clearly part of any concept of a professional service and is implied one way or another in the MRS code.

With a premium on meeting requirements, ISO 9000, not surprisingly, lays some emphasis on dealing with customer complaints and this will be mentioned again shortly (see under 'Solving problems'). Systems to ISO 9000 also encourage, although the Standard does not positively demand it, systematic monitoring of customer satisfaction. Since market research techniques are effective for such monitoring, it would be reasonable to expect market research agencies to be both equipped and ready to do this.

CONTROLLING THE WORK

As an industry, market research has tended to underplay 'doing' research. The professional researcher has tended to be more interested in the design bits and reporting than the mechanics of what happens in between. Yet, good project control makes all the difference between well and poorly conducted research and certainly to the profit made out of the work. Part of the reason for a lack of interest in project management is that this does not sit comfortably within the professional responsibility model of business quality. An ISO 9000 system, however, requires considerable thought and effort to be put into controlling work; into 'process control' in the terminology of the standard.

The implied or explicit requirements set out in ISO 9000, under process control, start with a need to understand and analyse the processes involved. In implementing such a system, this is an early step and one which is nearly always very beneficial in its own right. Examining what is actually done in a formal and logical way, and setting it all out, almost always has benefits, even if an ISO 9000 system is not in the end produced. Analysis will certainly identify weaknesses and obvious inefficiencies in working methods.

Following from analysis, there is a requirement in the Standard to define 'best ways' – methods of working which are considered most likely to lead to efficiency, minimise mistakes, ensure requirements are met and which, therefore, should be followed. Whether or not 'best ways' are set out formally, every agency will have some defined working methods; the staff do not decide afresh each day how everything will be done and nor is it likely that under any arrangements these methods will be entirely voluntary. More at issue, however, is the level of detail and generality of the defined working methods.

Arguably, the greater the level of detail written into procedures for controlling work, the greater the level of control. However, against this is the danger of rigidity; highly detailed procedures will not cover every possibility or circumstance or allow for changes in requirements or the way in which these are met. In implementing the Standard it is usually considered sufficient to limit defined 'best ways' to those which are considered critical; a satisfactory piece of work requires that such steps are consistently followed, while for other working methods, staff (or defined and appropriate staff) are assumed to exercise discretion. There is usually also an assumption of trained staff; working procedures are assumed to be followed by staff with the necessary skills and training.

The question of generality in working methods is linked to the level of detail. Defined working methods can cover all possible work that is ever likely to be undertaken, in which case they must of necessity be general and limited in detail, or they can relate to a specific type of work (or even one specific job) only, in which case there will need to be a wide range of documentation to span the full range of work and even then some will be found to not fit the system. For *ad hoc* research work, the better solution is usually to have fairly general defined methods leaving project managers etc to fill in the details, eg in written instructions relevant to the project which are given to other staff and departments involved. ISO 9000 in fact offers alternative methods of documenting working methods; procedures, quality plans and work instructions (see also below) and the choice between these links to the level of generality sought. Whatever is done in this respect, it should be remembered that a quality assurance system is there to assist efficient working and not prevent it. A certain indicator of a poor system is where a client requirement cannot be met because 'the system does not allow it'. This, in my experience, is not that uncommon in business generally.

Controlling work is also about ensuring that adequate resources to deliver the work are available. This also touches on design and meeting requirements since the Standard covers the need to be sure that the company can actually deliver and, therefore, has the resources available. Generally speaking, physical resources are not a major issue in market research; special plant and equipment is not normally needed and where it is (eg computing, venues etc) it can be bought in as required. What is often at issue is staffing, both in terms of numbers and their skills. To some extent these can also be bought in *ad hoc* but not always or for all tasks.

The staff numbers issue is a particular problem in *ad hoc* research where at the proposal stage the research design and the quoted time-table imply certain staff resources which at that particular point in time were available. Come commission, however, and this may be at some unpredictable time well after tendering, the situation may have totally changed. Attempting to solve this problem is a strategic management issue, usually regarded as well outside the scope of any quality system. Broadly, the choice is to staff-up for an assumed level of future *ad hoc* commissions and risk under-used capacity or be staffed for the current work loads and deal with crisis peaks as best you can. Between these choices there is no easy solution and this illustrates an important point; quality systems do not work in isolation from the business as a whole and planning and operating one has to be integrated with general business planning.

The Standard does have specific requirements in relation to training; identification of these needs and ensuring that these are met. However, since market research is so staff-skill dependent it is hard to imagine any agency falling short of the rather limited requirements, in this respect, as set out in ISO 9000. Because, in practice, very little has to be done in relation to training to meet the Standard, some businesses, including research agencies, have chosen to match their activities in this area to the more specific standard of Investors in People (IiP) which sits quite well with ISO 9000. However, IiP can be sought without ISO 9000 and some consider this a more useful approach although it clearly does not address all the other aspects of quality assurance covered by ISO 9000. Few, though, would advocate implementing both ISO 9000 and IiP at the same time; a bad case of management indigestion is the likely result.

Purchasing is also an aspect of controlling work. It is clearly pointless developing all sorts of procedures for internal staff if any rubbish can be bought in. ISO 9000 requires purchasing to be controlled, but adequate mechanisms – a controlled supplier list and written orders – are unlikely to be either difficult to follow in a market research company or be regarded as other than good business sense. Formalising what may be already recognised good practice will help ensure consistency and constant application; a member of staff will be less likely to place an order with a dubious subcontractor and with written orders it is less likely that a supplier will deliver something different to what is required.

A more problematical ISO 9000 requirement in relation to purchasing is 'receiving inspection'; the need to establish whether supplies are up to the required specification. In the case of manufacturing businesses, the supplies are likely to be mainly materials which can be subject to a variety of physical checks and tests. In market research, however, checking whatever is delivered – eg tabulations, completed questionnaires etc – may identify some sorts of problems (eg poor labelling) but will certainly not indicate whether the work that has gone into it is up to standard. However, some of these sort of problems also exist in relation to work done in-house and the Standard is sufficiently loose in this respect to allow implementation in a way practical for a service business such as market research. The difficulty of carrying out meaningful 'receiving inspection' also reinforces the need to select good suppliers, and the methods* used by these companies to ensure the quality of their own output may be a relevant criterion. So might be conformity to recognised industry service standards such as IQCS or MRQSA.

VERIFICATION AND CHECKING

Testing and inspection of outputs is really a feature of quality control rather than intrinsic to quality assurance, where the aim should rather be to obviate errors in the first place. In practice, however, quality assurance always incorporates some level of testing and inspection and this is a requirement of ISO 9000. However, the nature, number and frequency of testing and inspection are left to the implementing company which cannot be faulted (against the Standard) if none are included at any specific process stages. If the inspection is not useful, do not do it.

In market research work there is the practical problem that many types of error, which might occur, are not detectable by inspection after the

---

* ISO 9000 registration by the supplier could also be a relevant criterion but note that there is no requirement for ISO 9000 registered companies to restrict their purchasing to suppliers which also meet this standard.

event. If the interviewer did not, for example, rotate a question battery, it is very unlikely that any after-the-event check will identify this. There is, therefore, an added reason to do the work in the right way in the first place (the Standard refers to 'special processes' under 'process control' and this means the type of work which cannot be checked after the event). However, some inspection in market research is appropriate and practical and broadly this falls into either the checking of the work of more junior by more senior staff or more formal 'verification' procedures. Although the methods of the latter are not intrinsically different to the former, it is perhaps more a matter that the nature of the checking is more of a specified and standard nature.

Checking of juniors' work by seniors is almost always present, whether or not a formal quality system is in place and is no more than common sense. As in other areas, the difference made by prescribing the checking levels in a system is that of one of consistency; where appropriate it should always be done. However, whose work is to be checked by whom, on what occasions and when, requires careful thought at the planning stage and this is an area where systems end up being too rigid. Whatever is decided must take account of the need not to delay subsequent processes and the likely availability of the checker – it is no good specifying that all proposals must be checked by a director if all directors are usually out with clients. It should also be recognised that who checks whom is a politically and emotionally charged issue.

Verification type checking is usually applied to the more 'mechanical' processes, data collection and data processing, and may include such as 'back-checking' face-to-face interviews, 'silent monitoring' of phone interviews, editing of completed questionnaires and double 'punching' at data entry. The principles of doing these sorts of checks and who does it, is seldom a major issue – largely no doubt because the initial work is done by staff of too low a status to make a fuss. What is more problematical is the specific nature of the verification and how much of it should be done. The industry standards (IQCS and MRQSA) provide some minimum levels in these respects but are controversial.

SOLVING PROBLEMS

A very important requirement of ISO 9000 is to have effective mechanisms in place to identify problems and find ways of solving them so that they do not recur. The main mechanism of problem identification is 'internal audits' with 'corrective and preventive action' taken to solve the identified problems (problems may arise in ways other than through internal auditing, eg complaints from clients). Problem solving is meant to be radical – to get at the deep cause – rather than a patching-up exercise to get over the immediate crisis. Thus the organisation as a whole is meant to learn from its mistakes. The problems identified and solved may have arisen from the quality system (which may, therefore, need amending*) or from the operation of the processes themselves (in which case the quality system may need extending to cover the specific aspect of the process). A by-product of the investigation of problems and coming up with solutions is staff involvement in quality issues and business problems generally. Incidentally, the terminology of 'corrective and preventive' actions, used in ISO 9000, is not enticing (unless you are of a particular bent) and there is no reason why the activity should not be given a better name internally, eg 'Quality Improvement Opportunity' is used by at least one research company.

It is hard to imagine that anyone in market research (or elsewhere) will argue that identifying problems and finding long term solutions is either unnecessary or a bad idea. And of course this might get done anyway without formal procedures, but often it will not be done regularly. Again, a formal quality system offers the advantages of consistency and constancy and increases the chance of long-term quality improvement. As argued in the last chapter, if these aspects of quality assurance are pursued with vigour, the TQM aims of constant improvement and customer delight can be approached through a quality system. It may be claimed that the formality of such as internal audits and corrective actions is all very well in theory, but in practice there is seldom time to follow the procedures or follow them in more than a lip-service way. However, as Deming has said – 'how come you have enough time to make mistakes but not to solve them'. In the long run solving problems must be efficient.

MANAGEMENT

ISO 9000 is a model for managing quality and management involvement is essential. A quality system cannot be made the sole responsibility of a quality manager (although some of the detailed administration of elements of it can be left to him or her) with the board left to get on with the 'more important' things in life. If quality is not thought sufficiently important to involve senior management, there is no point in having a quality system. What is called for from management is commitment, leading by example and some specific action.

---

* But not always or even usually. Often it is more a matter of getting staff to follow a perfectly good and established procedure to avoid future recurrence of the problem.

It is the management's job to encourage commitment to a quality system and this requires more than putting up copies of a finely worded quality policy around the offices (ISO 9000 does require such a policy statement). My own view, in this respect, is that the actual policy is never as displayed and it is better that everyone understands the underlying thinking than to rely on a mere form of words which inevitably become trite.

Also, far more motivating for staff is that the boss follows the system – if he or she sends written orders to Field and DP and uses the project checklist etc (assuming that all this is part of the system). If he or she does not use the system, how can it be much good?

Specific management action as prescribed in ISO 9000 is limited to management review (around four meetings a year – possibly combined with such as a board meeting – to discuss the working of the quality system is regarded as generally satisfactory for a smaller company) and ensuring that one of the management team takes administrative responsibility as the 'management representative'. The degree of formality in these arrangements can fit the culture and size of the company.

The requirements relating to management in ISO 9000 raise no special problems for a market research company compared to any other business. Because most agencies are small business, there is always the problem of finding time for management work of any sort and in any area; the principals are fully committed to being practising researchers. There is no simple solution to this and again the problems are not peculiar to market research. A balance has to be struck and where this should be may depend on the growth objectives of the businesses. A growing business may be critically dependent on the input of the senior staff in day-to-day work but the growth will falter unless time is found for managing the business as a whole. To put the matter the other way round, many businesses fail to expand above a very small level because no time is found for the general rather than specific. That is fine if that is what the parties involved really want.

DOCUMENTS AND RECORDS

Yes, I have left this aspect of ISO 9000 to last because it is widely seen as the most negative. All the adverse publicity about ISO 9000/BS 5750 (and there used to be a lot) has tended to home in on form filling and unproductive bureaucracy. Two points to make right away are that most of such problems are self-inflicted and caused by poor system design and that secondly, market research is at least at some advantage compared to ruder businesses. Drafting documents and designing forms is, after all, our stock in trade.

The need for a documented quality system is a very specific requirement of ISO 9000 and cannot be avoided. As a minimum there needs to
be a quality manual which relates the requirements of the Standard
to the layout of the particular system (once drafted, this document is of
limited use) and a procedure manual. For day-to-day purposes the documented system is a collection of procedures and associated record
systems. The system can be extended with quality plans and work instructions although these are by no means essential or always appropriate.
The documented system must also be kept updated and controlled,
bearing in mind that it will need revising from time to time – the principle is that all staff following a process work to the same version of a
procedure or instruction. Planning all this and drafting something that
is satisfactory takes time and there must also be a lesser and spasmodic
input for revisions. However, this work is largely one-off and can be aided
by outside consultants or other short term assistance (although not to the
exclusion of management and staff involvement). Also, as I have indicated, it is not work outside the skills of most research staff. Anyone who
can plan, control and report on a sizeable *ad hoc* project is certainly
capable, after a little coaching, of putting together a satisfactory documented quality system.

Records are, however, potentially more of a problem. Once forms or
similar are designed-in they must be completed whenever specified in the
system. The chore is ongoing, forever and often apparently pointless. In
many cases, problems of this sort can be traced back to overenthusiasm
when the system was designed; it was forgotten that the forms have to be
used as well as designed.

Records arising from the process covered by a quality system* should
serve one of two purposes only; to establish which processes have been
carried out during a particular project (and, therefore, showing where the
job is up to) and recording the results of checks, tests and inspections.
Clearly, control of work necessitates knowing what has been done in a
job to date and this is particularly important in a process such as market
research where any tangible product has few indications of the process.
A record of the processes can take various forms, although often the
working documents necessarily produced by the process itself (eg questionnaire masters, reports etc) and, where required, instruction sheets
passed to other members of staff, can themselves be the record. Another
effective tool is a project checklist with each process signed off when

---

* There is also a need for records arising from the administration of the quality
system (eg audit reports). But this type of record is less of a problem if only because
the staff involved are often selected because they are methodical enough to keep
files etc in order.

completed and neither this nor using process-intrinsic documents need generate significant 'busy' work.

Records of checks, tests and inspections do require documentation which would not otherwise be needed. However, there is no point in doing the checking if there is no record of what was found; if the record is of no practical use then neither is the check, and it should be taken out of the system (although it might be imposed from outside, eg from IQCS or MRQSA). As I pointed out earlier, ISO 9000 does not require any specific tests or checks and it is up to the implementer to do what is useful and appropriate.

At some later point, I will make the point that procedures should be auditable and, therefore, produce some record that they have been followed. However, the converse is not true. A need for a record should not be built into a system just to make it auditable; if the record has no intrinsic value there is something wrong with the procedure.

Records need to be related to specific projects' 'product identification' and the use of job numbers or similar identification methods is hardly radical in market research. Like them or not, above a certain size of operation they just seem inevitable. The numbers have to be used on the records, but again few market researchers will find this difficult to follow.

The standard also requires that the records are adequately filed and stored; there is no point to them if you cannot find them. In the case of current market research jobs, this generally means an active job file for current projects which is archived once complete. Again, there is little new in job files and the effect of ISO 9000 is likely to be a positive one of making the file rather more ordered and systematic (at least one major research company considered this to be justification enough for implementing the Standard). However, beware of 'dress' files kept by project managers just for the benefit of auditors; this is a symptom of playing at ISO 9000 rather than implementing an effective quality system.

Records can of course be electronic, as can the system documentation (the Standard recognises this). Where computer networks are well established and adequately supported there is everything to be said for this approach, but there is a need to consider the security of electronic quality records with back-ups and virus protection etc. However, the same applies, if not more so, to process records as well – data processing files etc.

IS IT ALL WORTHWHILE?

Starting from scratch, developing a formal quality assurance system will be a major project and operating one will require some change in an organisation's culture. Seeking certification to ISO 9000 will also impose a further burden. All this will involve some costs. There has to be, there-fore, some good reason for doing all this. Clearly we should expect to find benefits of an ISO 9000 system in relation to quality and, linked to this, efficiency. However, ISO 9000 is also about perceived as well as actual quality and benefits of this sort are first considered.

Being assessed to ISO 9000, a widely recognised international standard throughout the business world, undoubtedly has value. Just having the certificate is the main or even only reason why some organisations (not necessarily market research agencies) have gone through the process of assessment. One factor in this is that in one way or another it is thought essential to be certified to ISO 9000 in order to keep business and, there-fore, like it or not, there is no real choice. Certainly some companies do operate a policy which favours or even demands ISO 9000 status from its main suppliers. In the vehicle industry this is well established, as it is in utilities. However, this has generally applied to manufacturing supplies and rather less for services although, of course, until service suppliers began to take up ISO 9000, customers had practical difficulties. In market research, some large buyers have indicated that an ISO 9000 supply policy would be also applied but to my knowledge this has very rarely been enforced and lack of certification has not led to significant lost business. Possibly research buyers will in future become more restrictive in their buying policy but this could also be as a result of agencies, for whatever reason, taking up ISO 9000; if nearly all the major research companies are certified, those which are not may be seen, no doubt wrongly, to be ill prepared to take on major contracts and could start losing business as a result. However, this has not happened yet and may never come about.

There are, however, other and more positive arguments for having ISO 9000 certification rather than the defensive 'must have' reason. One way or another, ISO 9000 is likely to be perceived as a positive statement about a research company's commitment to quality and client service. Not all potential clients will be impressed but some will be and, along with other factors, will be a reason for favouring an agency which registered to ISO 9000. This may be particularly the case in the international market. Because ISO 9000 is an international standard, overseas clients may feel more confident in a certified agency. Business may not be won just for this reason, but it will help, even though it may never be possible to accu-rately quantify this effect. More diffusely, ISO 9000 certification may also assist the general image building of an agency and in this way contribute to its long-term growth. A company with ISO 9000 may just seem to have set its sights higher and be moving up in the business. Finally, a 'system' approach can also assist when the owners come to sell it. Market research is recognised as people business, but this can be a problem in disposal; what is left of the business when the principals have gone with their proceeds? With both effective and credible systems in place and certification to prove this, the business may seem just a little more tangible.

The above arguments for ISO 9000 are really nothing to do with objectively achieving quality even if they do affect client perceptions. I shall now turn, therefore, to the more fundamental arguments which are more about having an effective quality assurance system regardless of whether or not it is certified. As discussed previously, delivering quality concerns commitment, process and people, so how does an ISO 9000 system measure up in these respects?

Any effect on commitment is arguably no more than reinforcement. Having a system in place is a symbol of commitment to a company's staff (it may be represented with framed policy statements and the like). Having registration is also a form of public commitment since the system is independently scrutinised. This will have a reinforcement effect internally through the prospect of assessment and later surveillance visits from the certification body. A good ISO 9000 system also needs real staff involvement, both in setting it up and in running it. This should help make everyone quality conscious and committed and an ISO 9000 system can assist in making the management's objective into a whole-company matter.

However, there is a circular aspect to commitment and ISO 9000. There may be positive effects, but the system itself requires commitment as a prior condition of successful implementation; commitment from senior managers and commitment from staff generally. Without this commitment the system either will not work at all or at only at a very low level. This can often be the result where the primary or only objective is certification for its own sake. Another aspect of commitment is that the level of quality as excellence to be sought must be defined from outside the quality system. Quality assurance can certainly assist in making improvements but what standards of work are 'right' or minimally right must be defined professionally or in conformance to accepted industry standards such as IQCS or MRQSA. An ISO 9000 system has, therefore, a strong linkage with commitment but it is a two-way process and some commitment to quality and standards of quality has to be injected from outside the system.

The effect on the process aspect of quality is obviously crucial to any case for an ISO 9000 system since it is about managing the aspects of the processes which effect or deliver quality. The aim in process is to ensure that requirements, especially client requirements, are met and that standards of quality are also met whether these are industry recognised (eg IQCS and MRQSA), professional or defined internally. It is not hard to profess commitment to all this, but the need is for constancy and consistency; to meet requirements and standards all the time and not just when there is nothing more pressing on the agenda. None of this will happen of its own accord and in some way it must be managed.

In a very small operation, this management can be very informal and the professional responsibility model of quality may be enough. However, above a quite low level of organisational size, a more formal method of managing the process to deliver quality will become essential. Inevitably there will be more or less formal ways of managing projects to ensure the work is right and the service to the client as satisfactory as possible. Controls of some sort will have to be introduced to ensure this and in one form or another these will get written down. The result will be a form of quality assurance 'system' but it will be haphazard and rather chaotic; the working rules will be followed most of the time but not always; sometimes it will be hit and miss. In some situations the 'right way' will be uncertain, so 'bad ways' will be followed by default. The only remedy for all this is to formalise and integrate the implicit system into a coherent whole. Assuming that more than just checking will be entailed (and this is not enough in market research) the system that results will be some version of quality assurance whether or not it is recognised as such. Quality assurance systems are, therefore, almost an inevitable outcome of growth; quality has to be managed and systems are needed to manage it.

The quality assurance system that is developed can be wholly home grown. But why reinvent the wheel? ISO 9000 is a standard defining key features of successful quality assurance and incorporates the collective wisdom of many organisations and individual managers; it has been proven throughout the business world. Nor is it too inflexible to meet the 'special' nature of market research; on the contrary, it is a sufficiently general system to meet the needs of any type of business. In one form or another, all the mechanisms of the model will be needed in an effective quality system. This includes those which assist problem solving and quality improvement although other approaches may be useful in this respect as well, eg TQM techniques such as quality circles, benchmarking etc which can sit alongside system methods. The argument is, therefore, why not use ISO 9000 as a model when the point is reached when a more formal operating system is a self-evident necessity? The only downside is that some of the particular requirements of the ISO 9000 models may seem onerous or ill-suited to market research but, as I shall show in the next chapter, a reasonable fit is possible in nearly all respects.

What then of ISO 9000 and people? The commitment side has already been discussed. Will the Standard help to improve the skills and ability of staff to deliver quality? In this respect, ISO 9000 is not particularly strong, with the subject covered under one of the shorter requirement headings ('Training'). As I will argue in the next chapter, this requirement can be met with only cursory lip service to training and skill building needs and any market research company will almost certainly wish to go further than just meeting the requirements of ISO 9000 in this respect.

The Investors in People Standard can be considered as a supplementary model (see Chapter 10).

In summary, therefore, I contend that the arguments for adopting the ISO 9000 model are strong; at least in companies above the very smallest. The case for seeking assessment and certification is rather different and more concerns the marketing of the business than its internal operation. Not that this is unimportant. In addition, however, the assessment process will assist the effective working of the system. The procedures incorporated may all be accepted as right and proper but without external scrutiny there will be some danger of slippage when things are hectic. Before long, without the need to satisfy an external body, using the system may be the exception rather than the rule. With the best of intentions and the greatest of commitment, we all sometimes need the policeman to help us be good.

7

ISO 9000 – in more detail

Having discussed the general principles of a quality assurance and ISO 9000 and the value of this approach to quality, I shall now discuss what is required to implement this standard and especially, in more detail, the requirements which must be met to match up to the ISO 9001 or 9002 models.

ISO 9000 REQUIREMENTS

The ISO 9001 model sets out requirements under 20 main headings and ISO 9002* under 19. The only difference between the two models is that ISO 9001 includes requirements for design and ISO 9002 omits these. I shall, therefore, confine discussion to the ISO 9001 model and, as already noted, most market research companies implementing ISO 9000 have chosen the ISO 9001 model.

The headings and numbering of ISO 9001 follow a certain logic but its basis is by no means very obvious without a full understanding of the whole model. In Figure 7.1 the headings are rearranged into four blocks, with the central one covering the requirements that directly affect the market research process and the blocks to the left and right having a

---

* ISO 9003 covers only twelve headings and is really a model for quality control rather than quality assurance; no market research company has shown or is likely to show any interest in ISO 9003. The ISO 9000 series also covers other documents but in all cases these are for guidance and explanation and are not models to implement.

supporting role. The implications of each requirement heading (listed in Figure 7.1) in a market research business will now be examined. However – be warned – only a précis is attempted; for a fuller explanation of each heading, read the Standard itself (BSI 1994) or publications explaining what it all means (eg Jackson and Ashton, 1993, 1995a) and for a definitive translation of the requirements to market research see the MRQSA guidelines document (MRQSA, 1995).

RESEARCH PROCESS REQUIREMENTS

Ten of the 20 requirements of ISO 9000 directly relate to the research process and in the figure they are arranged in the logic of research rather than by their numerical designation.

Design

4.4 Design control (ISO 9001 only)

As already mentioned, the requirements in relation to design are demanding and do not fit easily into market research practice. However, with a bit of hammering and bending a reasonable and workable join can be made. It is generally accepted that design covers three main areas in market research; the basic research design including a methodology (eg interview method, type of samples, their size and structure etc) and which is normally set out in a client proposal, the design of questionnaires and discussion guides and the design of branded research methods* to meet the needs of a number of clients. That the above is defined as design and other activities such as detailed sampling plans, drafting reports and presentations etc are not, is, admittedly, arbitrary. However, research activities which are not design are within the scope of other process requirements so are not outside the scope of the ISO 9001 model. Nor do all research services involve design (as defined); where the client specifies the methodology in some detail and drafts the questionnaire, the research agency can be assumed to be not involved in design work (and if all work is of this sort – eg a field and tab operation – ISO 9002 rather than 9001 may be appropriate).

Design work is required to be carried out in a controlled way, with formal procedures applied and which should cover planning the work, allocating staff to do it, defining what is required to do the design work

---

* Anyone developing a serious branded research product is likely to put enough effort into the work, and sufficiently document it, to meet the requirements of the Standard and this type of design is not discussed any further.

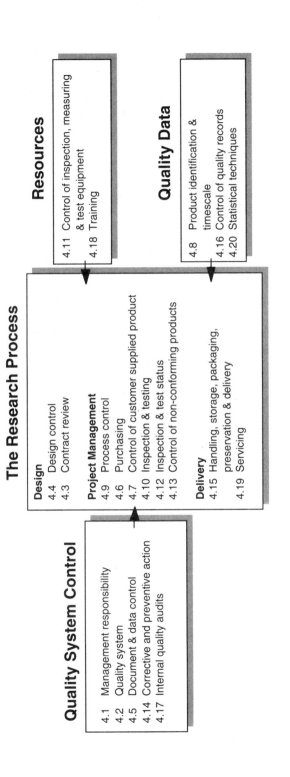

Figure 7.1 *Requirements of ISO 9001 in market research*

and documenting the results. Design work must also, to meet the Standard, be reviewed, verified and validated and if changes are made to an initial design these must be controlled. To anyone who has been happily writing successful proposals for years, all this will seem either alarming or unnecessary.

The difficulty with the requirements for planning design work (*4.4.2 Design and Development Planning*), when applied to market research, is that planning and doing a proposal or questionnaire are normally one and the same and done by the one person. There needs to be some defined mechanism for deciding who is capable and should do the work and the practical solution is typically to have the decision made by someone of sufficient seniority (eg a director, partner etc) who can be expected to make a sensible decision – he or she could of course select himself or herself to do the work. This decision may also cover who else in the company (*4.4.3 Organisational and Technical Interfaces*) should be consulted in the work, or general procedures may define this. However, depending on the specific job or even the type of work generally carried out, no one else apart from the proposal writer or questionnaire drafter may need to be involved.

The major design input (*4.4.4 Design Input*) will be the client's requirements; these must be documented to meet the Standard but briefing notes either taken in meetings or received from a client or set out as part of the proposal itself adequately achieves this and is part of normal research practice. At the questionnaire stage the proposal is normally the documented input. Procedures should also cover how the proposal or questionnaire is documented (*4.4.5 Design Output*) but there is no need to be rigid; different clients and jobs have different needs in terms of proposal format and a letter or even a note of a verbal quotation might be appropriate. Standardisation in questionnaire layout may, however, offer some real efficiencies. The procedures should also cover where the proposal or questionnaire drafts are to be kept and filed and some formality here usually gives benefits; at least the documents are less likely to be lost.

At its simplest, design review (*4.4.6 Design Review*) is a matter of deciding whether the design produced actually meets what is required; not a bad thing to do. It may be considered enough that this is done solely by the person drafting the proposal or questionnaire, but the involvement of others is normally beneficial although the seniority of the drafter may be the deciding factor. In designing physical products, verification of designs (*4.4.7 Design Verification*) may include highly technical work including tests and recalculations. In market research, verification may be thought of as part of the review stage and include considering whether the design matches requirements on the basis of professional knowledge (eg will the sample size produce results within acceptable confidence limits?) and reference to previously undertaken work where the same or similar methods worked. In questionnaire design work, verification might include checking wording for conformity to established norms. Pilot interviews are also a form of effective verification. Verification is undoubtedly better done if someone other than the initial designer is involved but if this is either impractical (eg in a small agency no one else may be available) or not appropriate (eg no one else has the experience of the subject area) then drafter-only verification will suffice.

Validation (*4.4.8 Design Validation*) is to do with establishing whether the design actually works. Client approval of proposals or questionnaires is deemed to be effective validation although to my mind this proves very little unless the client has some expert knowledge. Checks by staff in data collection or processing units can also be regarded as effective validation and so can comparisons of research results with other sources (eg previous surveys, desk research, client data etc) although considerable interpretation is usually required and such comparisons are seldom conclusive.

Research designs are often changed. An initial proposal is modified on commission and questionnaires typically go through several versions before they are used. The requirements here (*4.4.9 Design Changes*) are that the changes are reviewed (comparable to the review of the initial design), it is clear which version of a design document (proposal or questionnaire) is the latest – there are various techniques for this but none foolproof – and if the job is already underway, that staff involved are made aware of the changes and how these affect their own work.

Although, therefore, design control requirements of ISO 9001 seem demanding and difficult, in practice most agencies can probably adapt existing methods of working without massive or over-demanding changes. The over-riding need is one of knowing – and knowing after the event – what has gone into the design work, that the prescribed procedures have been followed and who has been involved.

4.3 Contract review

Where research design work is carried out, procedures to meet the requirements of Design Control will almost certainly meet the requirements under this heading although it may be considered good practice for someone with sufficient seniority and experience to review the commercial aspects of a proposal (costs and timing). However, the Standard does not really address this issue.

Where no design work is involved, the client's requirements and what is to be delivered should be specified and the documentation produced – quotation letters, faxes etc – should be reviewed for adequacy. Once the job is on, some form of written go-ahead is good practice although there is no need to require the client to send in a written order (unless this is considered commercially desirable and practical). Like design work, any changes made to the contract with the client on or after commission should be documented and staff involved in the project made aware of the changes.

In drafting procedures, an integrated approach to design control and contract review is usually best, with much the same steps followed whether or not the contract and proposal involves design work. At the questionnaire stage, contract review is not relevant.

Project management

Most of the other 'process' requirements of ISO 9001/2 can be thought of as part of project management and the implementation of these elements of a system should (and if done properly, will) make this more effective.

4.9 Process control

This requirement applies to all aspects of the research process other than design (where the equally or more rigorous requirements of Design Control apply). Process control includes; responsibility for managing the project (eg every job having a defined project manager) and defining 'best ways' for critical steps, usually in the form of procedures although quality plans and general work instructions can also be used (see shortly). Control also includes ensuring appropriate (suitably trained and skilled) staff are allocated to work and that they know what is required – and are if necessary given written instructions about what is to be done in the particular job. The progress of a job should also be easily established from such as a job checklist.

This requirement also covers the selection, availability and maintenance of suitable equipment. This certainly covers computer hardware and software, but also such as audio and video recorders and monitors. For most tasks, there is not likely to be any real issue about which equipment is suitable, although procedures may need to cover making sure that what is required to do the job is available when needed. How involved these procedures need to be depends on how big a problem such availability is, or is thought likely to be. Where the problems are at a low level, the procedures hardly need to be elaborate. The same principle applies to maintenance. A planned approach is required by the Standard but what is the likelihood that deterioration will affect quality? Generally computers work or they do not; they do not gradually go wrong. Also computer errors are often self-diagnosed and it may be sufficient to have adequate back-up and replacements if one unit goes down, without having regular and expensive maintenance carried out. In the case of other equipment, such as recorders, some back-up provision may be needed and individual machines may need testing before use.

4.6 Purchasing

Purchasing relates to things or services bought-in which affect the quality of research produced. Subcontracted fieldwork, data processing, sample generation and delivery services all clearly come into this category and so does the use of freelance specialist staff. More borderline are materials like stationery which although they form part of the delivery to the client may be considered to vary so little in quality that rigorous control is not needed. The purchasing of process equipment (eg computers) falls within the scope of this requirement but not infrastructure supplies (eg office cleaning, furniture etc). Procedures are needed to help ensure that what is bought is satisfactory as an input into the research process. The specific need is to control and evaluate suppliers; at the most basic, a list of approved suppliers and some formal method of evaluation to decide whether their service and what they deliver meets requirements. In practice, this will often amount to those dealing with the supplier making a judgement and recording their conclusions. The approved list should be reviewed at least annually, taking into account these evaluations. There will also need to be some way that new suppliers can be used such as through a probationary supplier list. Who decides which suppliers are on the approved or probationary list needs to be defined and, although this is not a requirement of the Standard, the procedures may sensibly cover who in the company can place orders, for what and for how much.

There is also a need under this heading to document purchases and at least for substantial amounts a written order is good commercial practice in any case. If it is considered satisfactory to place small orders by phone, there is no need to start placing written orders although there should be an internal record of what has been bought (eg a small-order log book). The system of evaluating suppliers can be usefully linked into an order form with a judgement of performance subsequently recorded on the file copy.

4.7 Control of customer supplied product

Material or services supplied by a customer for incorporation into the final output have a potential effect on quality and the Standard has a specific heading covering these circumstances. In market research, examples of customer supplied product include; test products (eg for placement or hall test), prompt material, draft questionnaires (particularly relevant in field and tab work) and all types of information. The two requirements are to keep the material safe and check that it is as required. Keeping

119

material safe may need to take account of its confidential nature and what is to be done with it once the work ends. Procedures are needed to cover this but will not usually need to be either extensive or detailed.

4.10 Inspection and testing

As already discussed, the only relevant form of inspection and testing in market research in most cases is checking, with the checker's opinion the basis of whether the work passes or fails. Usually the checker is more senior to the checked. More formalised inspection or verification includes double punching or similar in data entry and back-checking or monitoring in fieldwork. Appropriate techniques and methods of this will be considered in separate chapters (Chapter 8 and Chapter 9). Even with these more formal approaches, however, the inspection may have a more subjective element than would be acceptable with physical products. Furthermore, and also as already discussed, the quality of some aspects of market research work cannot be determined by examining any sort of final product; good or poor research may not look any different in a final report, and even the adequacy of some research processes may be difficult to check once they are finished.

Procedures are required to specify when, where, how and by whom checking or other inspection and testing should be carried out. It must be emphasised that the nature of this work and at which specific points in the process it is carried out is almost entirely a matter for the company implementing the standard. The Standard does refer to inspection and testing in three stages, receiving, in-process and final, but this still leaves much open in practice. The only limitations on this freedom to self-specify the level and nature of inspection and testing is that some checking is essential to meet the Standard and if no checks are carried out at obviously critical points, the decision to do nothing may have to be defended (assuming the system is to be assessed). This lack of prescription was one of the main criticisms of ISO 9000 applied to market research. This will be fully discussed elsewhere, but for now it is enough to state that as a consequence of this criticism, the newly developed service standards for the market research process as set by MRQSA (and IQCS) effectively set out a minimum level and nature of checking. However, this only has any force if the company implementing ISO 9000 chooses to also incorporate MRQSA/IQCS standards.

As I have just mentioned, ISO 9001/9002 refers to a need for inspection and testing on receiving deliveries from suppliers, in-process and at a final stage. Most meaningful checking and verification in market research is undertaken at various in-process stages. Questionnaire printing, the completeness of material dispatched to interviewers, the back-checking of their work, editing completed questionnaires, draft code-frames, coding and data entry, data processing programmes and output and reports and presentations are all points in a job where checking and verification may be appropriate. Receiving inspection is more difficult since at least some of the features of the material or service supplied may not be testable after delivery – fieldwork is largely in this category. Also, although some sorts of bought-in inputs might in principle be checkable, it may not be convenient or practical to do so. The Standard allows the nature of receiving inspection and testing (and by implication its absence) to be determined by evidence of the supplier's capability and performance. The work of a fieldwork agency, for example, may be considered to be satisfactory without any sort of testing if the company concerned is a member of IQCS. There is also a problem in carrying out final inspection and testing in market research. Once all the in-process checks have been completed, what else can be done? The client's satisfaction can be established but this is a rather different (but none the less valuable) sort of process. The project manager can also 'sign off' the job to confirm everything appropriate has been done.

There is no point in testing and inspection if the results are not recorded, and the Standard requires this. Nor is there any point if no action is taken on the basis of the outcome of testing; if in principal nothing useful can be done, regardless of the results, or in practice the results are invariably satisfactory, the activity is almost certainly pointless and not worth carrying out. Where in-process checks are unsatisfactory the work should not pass on to further stages until the problems are rectified. However, in some cases – eg interviewer back-checking – the work will have passed on before test results are known; otherwise the work will be seriously delayed (and timeliness is likely to be a key requirement). In such cases, the faulty work will have to be traced through the subsequent processes and rectified; this could involve such as repunching data and rerunning tables and in the extreme the client may need telling that the output is suspect. Professional ethics should anyway require nothing less. The Standard requires that the product should not be delivered at all until final inspection and testing is complete. However, the nature of such tests in market research is often so nebulous that the requirement has little relevance; to be pettifogging, the final delivery can be deemed to have occurred once the final sign off has been made and this may be well after reports etc are delivered. But this achieves nothing in real quality terms.

4.12 Inspection and test status

All this requirement involves, in market research, is being able to know where in the process a job has reached, what tests have been carried out and the results of those tests. The records kept relating to a job (eg in a job file) will be sufficient to achieve this.

4.13 Control of non-conforming product

In market research, non-conforming product is faulty work; inadequately completed or suspect questionnaires, data entry batches with above acceptable error rates, the output from faulty data processing programming, reports needing correction etc. Once problems are identified, the work will need correcting before passing on to the next stage (or where this has happened, further remedial work may be needed). In some cases, material output (questionnaires, tabs etc) may need marking as faulty or be kept separate so that it is not mistaken for good work. Procedures are needed to ensure these things are done correctly and that records are made of problems which occur. The responsibility for decisions about remedial work should also be defined.

Delivery

4.15 Handling, storage, packaging, preservation and delivery

Because market research output is only partly tangible, this requirement heading can usually be addressed with few procedures and little difficulty. The physical handling and packaging of such as reports is hardly an issue although any delivery service used clearly needs to be reliable and safe; commercial sense will dictate this. Storage covers keeping all working documents and data relating to a project for defined periods (minimums are specified by MRQSA and in the MRS code) and how it is then disposed of should be specified.* Some documents will be kept for longer periods or forever and it may be desirable to have duplicates at another site. Data and reports may be in electronic form and special storage and back-up is likely to be required. The confidential nature of some data may need to be considered in deciding how and where they are to be kept. Obviously any storage system needs to allow for retrieval in a reasonable time.

Some types of test products may need special storage and handling, and especially foods. If this sort of work is undertaken, procedures should be in place to comply with health and safety legislation.

4.19 Servicing

Servicing after delivery, is of limited relevance in *ad hoc* market research; reports do not break down after delivery. However, the resources and

---

*   The storage of computer data and records from which these data are taken is covered by the Data Protection Act although there is little that is specific in this legislation.

ability to respond to client queries post delivery (for perhaps a defined period) is a need that often must be met. The adequate filing of working documents and reports etc may suffice (and relate to other aspects of project management). Continuous research may have more demanding requirements for client servicing but what is appropriate should be clear on commercial grounds. Keeping in touch with past clients can also be thought of as servicing and to formalise how this is done (and ensure it is) should have a measurable pay-off.

RESOURCES AND QUALITY DATA

The requirements shown in the right hand blocks in Figure 7.1 relate to activities which have a supporting role rather than being part of the research process itself.

4.11 Control of inspection, measuring and testing equipment

The type of tests carried out in manufacturing often require the use of measuring equipment – scales, gauges, meters etc – and such equipment may also be part of the process itself. The use of any such equipment is found in only some specialised areas of market research – eg scales for checking print colour where this is critical, thermometers used for the storage of test frozen food. Most research agencies will be able realistically to claim that they have no such equipment in use and that, therefore, this requirement of the Standard cannot be pratically applied. If such equipment is in use, quite extensive and detailed procedures are required.

4.18 Training

Few research companies will be unaware that success is wholly dependent on the skills of their staff and most will already carry out training programmes which are quite adequate to meet the requirements of ISO 9000. Training should include all staff – professional and others, including interviewers (eg to the standard specified by IQCS) and the operation of the quality system as well as research and process skills. The level of training needed in the quality system will depend on individuals' roles: internal auditors and the management representative will need more than the basic understanding required by all staff working the new system. The training requirements of new recruits also need to be covered.

The specific requirements in relation to training are threefold: some means of establishing staff training needs, ensuring that the training required is carried out; and keeping a record of both needs identified and training received. The identification of needs can be successfully linked to an appraisal system. These requirements are not demanding; it would be perfectly possible to meet their letter by a manager having a five-minute meeting with each member of staff, once a year, and on this basis, concluding that no training at all is needed in the current year. However, this would achieve nothing for quality and all companies need to make training and skills a major concern. Investors in People (IiP) provides a far more demanding standard to structure training and it fits well with ISO 9000 (meeting IiP more than satisfies ISO 9000). IiP is discussed in detail in Chapter 10.

4.8 Product identification and traceability

This requirement is about the need to be able to trace back to the processes carried out in a particular project; the steps followed, who worked on it, checks carried out etc. This requirement is simply met by a job numbering system and ensuring that this number is included in all records relating to the particular job. While job numbers are often difficult to remember and work with, it is hard to think of any better system of unique identification. If any volume of work is carried out and irrespective of ISO 9000, nearly all research companies use some form of job numbering. A procedure and record system is needed to ensure that each job is given a unique job number.

4.16 Control of quality records

Records produced as a result of the quality system – eg results of checking, internal audit reports etc – need to be kept in such a way that they can be retrieved and used to establish that the quality system is working and to help identify quality problems. Most of these records will be kept in project files and can be regarded for this purpose as no different to the working papers and data produced in project. Procedures should describe the system for keeping records and define retention periods, which for all quality records needs to be at least a year. The records can, of course, be in electronic form and accessible only on-screen (such data need of course to be backed-up adequately and generally secure).

4.20 Statistical techniques

In manufacturing, statistical techniques are very often used for quality control purposes (statistical process control) and it is this sort of application to which this requirement refers. Statistical techniques are of course widely used in market research but as part of the research process itself rather than for quality control purposes. Where statistical methods are used in the research process, they should be covered by process control procedures although the wide variation in techniques appropriate to specific jobs may mean that detailed procedures are not practical and the choice of techniques etc has to be left to the discretion of qualified staff.

In most research operations the potential to use statistics in quality control is probably quite limited. Keeping a record of average error rates in such as back checking of interviewers, editing or data entry can be regarded as examples but are so simple that formal procedures are scarcely needed. Selecting the size of samples checked or verified in these processes may, however, suggest a need for more sophisticated methods and, if such techniques are to be used routinely, the application should be documented in procedures. However, any such exercise should be carried out only if useful action can be based on the results and certainly not just to meet the requirements of the Standard. If there are no useful applications, do not do anything in this respect.

QUALITY SYSTEM CONTROL

Nearly all the requirements of ISO 9001/2 discussed so far relate to activities which are likely to be familiar (if under different names) through running a market research business. The remaining five requirements of the Standard – those in the block on the left of Figure 7.1 – are rather different; they are requirements which only arise because a formal quality assurance system is to be implemented. Within this context they are, therefore, very important requirements of the Standard and are essential for the working of an effective quality system as per the ISO 9001/2 models. They also have a central role in assessment of a company. During site visits, the first step an external assessor usually takes is to check the records arising out of meeting these five requirements. However, the relevance of the five requirements goes beyond assessment since embedded in them are effective tools for maintaining and improving quality in an organisation. An indicator of whether a company takes the ISO 9000 models seriously or whether it is all just a matter of having the certificate, is whether or not activities such as management review, corrective action and internal auditing have substance rather than just form.

Implementation of the five requirements requires little in the way of translation to market research practice; it is much the same as in manufacturing or in other service businesses.

4.1 Management responsibility

The management of a company have to both take ultimate responsibility for implementation of a quality system to ISO 9000 and be actively involved in ensuring the system works effectively. Specifics within this heading include the need for a documented quality policy which should be available to and understood by all staff – the essentials can certainly be set out on one page. Responsibilities for the management, administration and operation of the quality system should also be formally defined and documented (again this can be kept short and succinct) and one individual should have the overall administrative responsibility for the working of the system – the Standard refers to a 'management representative'. He or she can go by any title but should be senior within the company, if not a member of the board.

The management of the company, collectively, need regularly to consider the effectiveness of the quality system – they need to carry out 'management reviews'. Quarterly is probably the minimum interval between these meetings but if convenient they can be held as part of general management or board meetings (although it may be useful to have non-directors attend, including of course the management representative if he or she is not a board member). Relevant topics at management reviews include; the results of internal auditing, any client complaints received, corrective actions raised and their outcome, effective implementation of the system, staff training needs in relation to it and the performance of suppliers. Minutes of the meetings are required. However, behind all of this should be the consideration of real quality issues and only if this substance is present will the system be really effective. As in other aspects, lip service and conformity to the form of the system will lead to an ISO 9000 certificate but not to many other benefits.

4.2 Quality system

ISO 9000 requires that there is a formal, documented quality system (this can be in electronic form) and that this is implemented effectively. As a minimum there are probably two elements to such a system; a quite short quality manual and a set of relevant procedures.

The quality manual is a statement of how the requirements of ISO 9001 or 9002 are applied within the particular organisation and describe to which part of the operation the system and the requirements of the Standard apply. The usual format to cover the latter is to list the Standard's major headings and cross-reference to the procedures. To meet ISO 9000, it is not essential to cover all processes of the business; finance and marketing for example do not really fall within the scope of the Standard. However if a quality system approach is considered effective, it ought to be applicable in these as well as the central processes and it may be thought better to take a broader rather than a narrower view of what the system should cover.

Procedures are constantly mentioned in the requirements of the standard and, day to day, the procedures are seen as the quality system (the quality manual, while essential, is not likely to be consulted regularly).

Procedures document the essential steps in processes and once agreed and implemented are mandatory; staff should always work to them in relevant applications and they should, therefore, be both easy to follow and practical. Usually they apply to general processes carried out regardless of the particular project (although of course some processes may not apply to a particular job). Effective procedures should be written around the structure and sequence of processes of the particular company rather than the Standard; all requirements of the Standard must be covered but in a form which suits the unique circumstances of the particular business. Incidentally, procedures are required for implementing the requirements of quality system control; management review, document control, corrective actions and internal audits; even procedures for procedures are needed. Further comments on procedures and how to develop them are made below and more fully in Chapter 12.

As I have mentioned, procedures apply to general processes and most companies will consider that there is no need to formally document how the aims of the quality system will be met in specific jobs apart from such as written instructions passed to members of the project team. However, two other sorts of system documentation which can be considered (in effect use of them is voluntary in relation to the Standard) are quality plans and work instructions. Quality plans are typically used for one-offs; projects which do not fit the normal operations of the business or which are perhaps unusually large (preparing a quality plan is unlikely to be considered for a project which is not substantial). Such documents might also be thought useful in developing major branded research products. The contents of quality plans are likely to mirror procedures and will very likely cross reference to them.

Work instructions can be thought of as fairly detailed 'recipes' applied to a particular product and one which is regularly produced. In market research, such instructions might usefully be written for continuous projects which are carried out in the same way repeatedly or for omnibus surveys. A point about both quality plans and work instructions is that they must be 'controlled' – see below – and this may be a good reason for limiting their use (or not having them at all).

The documented quality system also includes forms and record sheets used in operating the procedures but these can be thought of as part of relevant procedures.

A final point in relation to the documented system is the requirement that it is implemented effectively. Providing the time can be made available and with a little tuition, few market research companies will have serious problems in producing the required documentation. Getting staff to work to procedures – all the time and every time – may, however, be found rather harder to achieve.

4.5 Document and data control

All this requirement implies is that quality system documentation should have some sort of official status and that all staff using it should work from the same and latest version. There are various techniques to achieve this and at least some of them should be used. Defined responsibility for authorising drafts (eg signed by the managing director), version numbering and dating new issues and maintaining lists of current versions are all useful ways of ensuring document control. The main enemies of control are the inevitable need to change documentation (it is then that there is a danger of old and new versions being in circulation) and that all staff need access to the documentation or at least the parts relevant to their work. Without control being exercised, staff are very likely to introduce chaos into the system. Electronic documentation often gives better control; with everyone accessing procedures etc on a network, there needs to be only this single and up-to-date version.

Effective document control can be achieved by common sense but it is something that external assessors consider to be very important – companies fail assessment just because their system documentation is in a mess.

4.14 Corrective and preventive action

This requirement is about solving quality problems, with an emphasis on ensuring the problem does not recur. Problems may arise and can be identified from customer complaints or in relation to the working or failure of the quality system itself or in the operation of processes. Such problems are obviously to do with quality but this of course includes inefficiencies as well.

Corrective action is about an immediate solution to a problem – eg a client complains, what can be done to make him or her less unhappy? After a report is written it is found that some of the data analysis was flawed, how can the report be corrected? What constitutes a problem is of course a matter for judgement. Individual errors identified during routine checks and corrected there and then would not normally be seen as a problem to be addressed through corrective action, but a rising error rate (and this would be a reason for monitoring it) would be.

Preventive action has a more long term aim than corrective action, with an emphasis on preventing recurrence; how can we be sure that the problem giving rise to the customer complaint will not happen again? How can we ensure the same sort of data processing errors do not happen next time? Of course, not all problems can be easily and permanently solved or it may be considered that the problem was a 'once off' with little chance of recurrence and that a radical solution is not needed. But even in such cases, the possibility of long-term solutions at least will have been considered.

Procedures are required to carry out corrective and preventive action and one set can cover both; both preventive and corrective solutions can be sought for every problem which is investigated. The procedures can also be given another title – such as the previously mentioned 'quality improvement opportunity'. Whatever it is called, it should describe how corrective and preventive actions are to be carried out within the company and what records are to be kept. The search for the cause of the problem and a proposed solution is carried out by an investigator, selected (eg by the management representative) to deal with the specific case or possibly those of a certain type. Other staff may well be consulted in investigation, along with any relevant records. The solution proposed may involve a change to the quality system and the related process or in how it is implemented, eg getting staff to follow procedures. The resulting report and proposed solution should be then considered and action agreed by the company's management (eg at a management review meeting) or the management representative may be given the discretion to act. Either way a timetable should be set for 'closing out' the corrective action.

A further aspect of corrective and preventive actions is that a wide range of staff should be involved as problem investigators or at least consulted in arriving at solutions. In this way everyone becomes quality improvement conscious and the wide range of talent is engaged. What corrective and preventive action should not be (despite its name) is a form of punishment. Staff who are 'bad' in quality terms should not have a corrective action 'raised against them'. However, staff who are having problems following part of the system should certainly be involved; perhaps some of the procedures just do not work.

4.17 Internal quality audits

And finally, the Standard requires problems to be positively sought out through internal auditing. Over a year or so, the operation of the whole quality system, throughout the whole organisation, should be audited to establish whether or not it is working effectively. To put it at its simplest, auditors establish – usually by checking the procedures – what should be done in a particular process and then compare this requirement with what actually happens in practice. Finding out what is happening may involve observing staff at work, asking them what they do and by looking at records produced through the operation of the system. Consulting these records is a particularly important part of an audit; they are considered to be a more 'objective' form of evidence. Where a difference between what ought to be and what is done is found, a 'non-conformity' exists and this should be dealt with by a corrective action, although whether or not one is raised may be at the discretion of the management representative. Where this happens it is appropriate to carry out a follow-up audit to establish whether the remedy has been effective.

There should be a procedure to describe the main steps in auditing* and who is responsible for managing the process (commonly the management representative). The work should be carried out by staff with some training and who are independent of the area to be audited. There are many courses available to train quality auditors but self-help and internal learning are acceptable – there are various books on the subject (eg Jackson and Ashton, 1995b). Independence from the area being audited can be achieved by 'cross-auditing'. Staff from one department audit another, or auditors can be drawn from departments whose operations are largely outside the quality system. Independent consultants can also be brought in to do the work. In all but the very largest research companies, auditing need only be a part time role; a team of two auditors working two days a month, for example, should be adequate to cover the system of a research company in the £2 million to £5 million range.

THE QUALITY SYSTEM CIRCLE

If the quality system control requirements of ISO 9001/2 are met, and met with the intention of achieving real benefits, they should link together as a very effective tool for maintaining and improving quality; for meeting requirements, satisfying and even delighting clients and ensuring that at least some level of quality as excellence is met or surpassed. Figure 7.2 illustrates this.

Quality problems are identified through internal audits and solutions proposed through corrective and preventive actions. The management review procedure may then lead to a decision to make changes and these may include changes to the documented quality system (with document control procedures ensuring that the system is kept in order). The implementation of the changes can then be established though a later audit and if necessary the whole circle followed again. Eventually the problem must be solved.

---

* See the Appendix for an example of auditing procedures. Note also that the auditing procedure should itself also be audited. I was once in trouble for not doing this. The reader is invited to think of how this can be done by an auditor who is both trained and independent.

Figure 7.2 *The quality system circle*

IMPLEMENTING ISO 9000

Implementing an ISO 9000 quality system involves a design and planning phase, a period of getting the new system to work effectively and then, if this is desired, being assessed by a recognised and independent body. Designing and planning an effective system will be a substantial project for any company but, if the commitment is there, well within the capability of any market research company. The fundamental skills needed will be in place and the additional technical knowledge needed is not so very great. An outside and specialist consultant can be of considerable help but such external assistance is by no means essential.

The system which is developed should of course meet the requirements of ISO 9001 or 9002 but also – and this is very important – match the unique circumstances and processes of the particular company. It should also be planned and structured so that it is practical and workable. There is also a strong case for incorporating MRQSA (and, therefore, IQCS) minimum standards for market research services; the resulting system will of course be seamless with respect to ISO 9000 and these industry standards. The requirements of these standards are discussed in the following two chapters.

A choice can be made at the design (and later) stage between a system which is just good enough to 'pass' ISO 9000 and one which will be really effective in achieving and maintaining quality. As discussed at the end of the last chapter, merely having the certificate has a value but perhaps not that much and all the work involved in developing and operating the system far outweighs any such benefit. Furthermore, there is not much difference in the effort required for an effective system compared to one which is merely certificate gaining. So the argument for doing it all properly (or not at all) seems overwhelming. However, a proper system does not need to be elaborate or overcomplex. It is better to start off with a minimum system which works and can be extended later, than an amazing structure which no one can understand or follow.

Some of the practical ways in which a quality system can be developed are described in Chapter 12 of this book.

ASSESSMENT

An effective quality system should be worth having whether or not it is assessed and a certificate awarded. However, nearly every company seriously developing and implementing a system to ISO 9001/2 will wish eventually to be assessed and, whatever else, assessment (and the system of follow-up continuous assessment) provides an added incentive to make the system work day in and day out. Assessors help us to be good.

Assessment should be arranged with a body accredited for ISO 9000 assessment in the market research field. The United Kingdom Accreditation Service (UKAS) sets standards for assessment bodies and, in effect, gives them a licence to offer assessment services. The UKAS will provide lists of approved assessment bodies; four are also approved by MRQSA to carry out assessment to this body's standards and this may be a sensible shortlist from which to make a choice (see Chapter 9). The bodies are commercial and charge for their services at management consultant rates. Once the quality system is working effectively, preliminary meetings with one or more of the assessment bodies can be arranged, quotations received and a choice made.

The initial assessment addresses two issues; first, does the documented system match the requirements of ISO 9001/2, and second, does the company follow its own system. The former issue may be addressed off-site by studying the system documentation, while the second will involve time on the company's site examining the operation of the full system in all relevant areas of the company. In principle, the work is no different to that carried out by well-trained internal auditing (carried out properly, internal auditing should indicate when the company is ready for assessment). If, as a result of the assessment, the company is considered to both have a system which meets the Standard and is followed in practice, an ISO 9000 certificate will be awarded. During the assessment, minor problems will almost certainly be found and a 'corrective action request' (CAR) will be raised which the company is expected to deal with and put right before the next assessment visit. However, such a request does not prevent the award of a certificate. Only if a whole group of procedures are not working or a major requirement of the Standard is not covered, will the company fail.

Initial assessment is followed by a programme of continuous surveillance visits carried out by the assessment body every six months. These are much shorter in duration and cover only part of the system and company, but over a two- to three-year cycle cover everything again completely. Minor problems found in these visits will result in a CAR being raised and a serious breakdown of the system could lead to loss of the ISO 9000 certificate.

How much does assessment cost for a market research company? No firm guidelines can be given, although for the smallest company, initial assessment (in 1996) might cost £500 and follow-up surveillance visits at £250 each or another £500 a year (there are two such visits a year). For a medium-sized operation – a turnover of up to £5 million per annum – the initial cost might be £2500 and surveillance £1500 per annum. For a large company the figures are much higher. Obviously, though, the costs of implementing ISO 9000 are more than this. There is the considerable internal time in design and planning and quite possibly consultant fees and together these will be far greater than the initial assessment charges. There is also an ongoing operating cost in administration of the system and training. However, by making quality everyone's concern, 'extra' inputs to the system should be minimised. Clearly, though, a judgement must be made of the likely costs and these weighed against the expected benefits.

8

Standards for data collection – IQCS

This and the next chapter are about formal quality standards for market research and the two bodies which exist to develop them and to provide the assessment or inspection services which enable companies to demonstrate compliance to the standards. The next chapter deals with standards and assessment arrangements of the Market Research Quality Standards Association (MRQSA), still a very recent initiative to deal with quality issues, but this chapter is concerned with the much longer established Interviewer Quality Control Scheme (IQCS), which, as the name suggests, is concerned with data collection or, more precisely, the role of interviewers.

INTERVIEWING PROBLEMS

Nearly all market research is based on data obtained by some form of primary data collection and whether or not this work is done well or badly has a very direct bearing on quality; on the 'rightness' of the results. No matter how sophisticated the research design, how technical the analysis and how brilliant the reporting, it will all be worthless if the interviewer's output is of an unacceptable standard. Garbage in, garbage out. In theory, the interviewing task is one of the easier parts of the research process; select respondents as per instructions, persuade them to cooperate then administer the questionnaire as directed. The formal skills to do this are generally considered to be limited, although a certain flair, it is acknowledged, is needed to gain cooperation (this tends to be undervalued by research executives because they may have never done any interviewing themselves). Yet, data collection and interviewing are problematical and to a large extent this is for structural reasons – how interviewers work and how they are employed.

Dealing for the moment just with 'field' interviewing – where respondents are interviewed face-to-face on the streets, in the home or at work – there is an inevitable limit to the control which the project manager or research designer can exercise over how an interviewer does her or his work. Interviewers work remotely from the agency office, very largely alone – direct supervision is only realistic for a small number of interviews in any programme – and their involvement in a project is confined to data collection. They do not generally know much of the overall objectives of the research or the wider methodology. Often, for good reason, they do not even know for whom the research is being carried out. Because of this restricted involvement, the skills of interviewers need be no more than is necessary to do interviews; they do not have to have fuller professional skills or for that matter professional status and commitment. To use full professionals for data collection is also almost always far too expensive within a commercial research context (there are exceptions; depth interviewing, piloting etc).

The above aspects of field interviewing potentially create some problems, but these are made more acute by the commercial structure in which interviewers are employed and work. If we look back 10 or 15 years, field interviewing was very largely structured as loose networks. Interviewers were 'self-employed' – paying their own taxes (or not), worked for local supervisors and had little direct contact with agency staff unless a project involved interviewer briefing in person. The supervisors were also largely self-employed and home based. Effectively they offered 'their girls' to agencies as and when required – it was the supervisor's job to put together a team to meet the fieldwork required in her own patch. Supervisors, like their interviewers, worked for a number of research companies, sometimes for many companies, although as in all businesses, some 'customers' would be bigger than others. Supervisors also tended to know counterparts in other areas and a start-up research company could quite quickly, and at virtually no cost, be able to claim a national field coverage; an interviewer on the Isle of Harris could always be located through a few network phone calls. Unless personal briefing was required, the small agency need never meet its interviewers face to face.

Obviously this structure was not conducive to the best quality fieldwork since agencies had almost no direct control over interviewers and could only hope that the work was done to an acceptable standard, whatever this might be. Interviewers also had little reason to have any feeling of loyalty to agencies since their 'employer' was a local supervisor who herself tended to have more regard for her own team than her clients, the agencies. In any dispute about quality of the output the supervisor, as likely as not, was defensive about 'her girls'. The tangible rewards offered to interviewers were low – unskilled or semi-skilled manual labour rates – but supervisors (who were exclusively drawn from interviewers) did a bit better. Interviewing was a part-time and spasmodic job and was generally regarded as offering 'pin money' rather than a living and, it was assumed, well suited middle class ladies with a bit of time on their hands.

This 'cottage' structure existed for economic reasons. Research companies themselves were almost entirely small businesses, but needed to be able to offer a capability of carrying out nationwide fieldwork. However, because job throughput in the typical agency was low, it was impossible to usefully employ local interviewing teams on any sort of continuous basis. Interviewers in Wolverhampton might be needed for a couple of weeks but then there would be no call for their services for a few months. Also, regardless of where fieldwork was needed, the total field requirement fluctuated with client commissions; some months there would be very little need for interviewers and some months too much. From the interviewers' point of view, continuity in employment necessitated working for several agencies, since none could offer reasonable workloads over the year. Also, as small companies, agencies lacked much in the way of in-house administration and were not, therefore, able to manage interviewers directly and were more than happy to turn over the responsibility to a local supervisor. The low rates offered to interviewers reflected supply and demand; with little or no training required to become an interviewer, supervisors could always find someone to take on work and the pay levels fed into the prices charged by agencies to clients; agencies could not afford to pay more than the going rate.

Is all this an exaggeration? Not much, and some market research is still organised in ways which are not drastically different to this picture. Market research still has a cottage industry part to it. However, there were always larger agencies with full-time supervisors and which could provide much of the interviewing team 'on the books' with reasonable continuity of work. Also, such companies ran interviewer training schemes and had some form of quality control in place to monitor interviewer performance. In this respect, smaller companies tended to live off the efforts of the larger ones which had training programmes. If interviewers had any training it was from larger companies. Over the last few years, larger companies have tended to do a larger proportion of all fieldwork and, therefore, more of it is done to the standards set by such companies. There have also been other developments which have favoured a closer contact and degree of control between agency and interviewer. One factor is that the tax authorities have stamped out self-employment of interviewers; agencies are required to account for tax and National Insurance and operate a proper payroll. With typically hundreds of interviewers on the books, this has created an additional administrative burden and some incentive to prune the field-force so that fewer interviewers are used, but each gets more work. Another factor is technology. Over the last few years, larger agencies have been moving from paper questionnaires to CAPI (computer assisted personal interviewing). As previously mentioned, this offers efficiency and quality benefits, but it also favours the use of smaller and more intensively worked fieldforces; laptop PCs cannot be handed out willy nilly even by the largest companies; the equipment is just too expensive. CAPI also necessitates additional training for interviewers.

There is also thought to have been some changes in the sociology of interviewers. Instead of middle aged, middle class ladies working for interest, love of humanity and pin money, fieldforces are now said to be largely staffed by single mothers dependent on the work for their daily bread. Certainly a caricature, but perhaps with a grain of truth. Such a trend might be expected to encourage interviewers to seek a more professional status and an increase in pay. However, such a trend may also lead to new quality problems; as interviewers seek larger earnings, shortcuts in work may be tempting.

Given that the research industry has had, and still has to some extent, this chaotic fieldwork structure, what are the implications for the quality of output? There is clearly the potential for problems and of two main sorts; interviewer variability and interviewer cheating.

Structured fieldwork assumes zero interviewer variability; the responses should be determined by the respondent and it should not matter who administers the interview. In practice, some level of interviewer variability is inevitable; minor variations in how respondents are selected, how they react to the interviewer, how the interviewer articulates questions, word stress and many other things – without the interviewer doing anything which can be classed as bad practice – will lead to some level of variability even though it may be possible to ignore the effect in practice. This inevitable level of variability will be aggravated by any poor practice such as not following respondent recruitment to the letter, quota squeezing (moving a borderline respondent to one classification or another as the need arises), prompting and leading respondents, not following questionnaire wording and inferring responses. There can be no doubt that such malpractices occur; often through poor training, or a desire to complete the work quickly, meet 'impossible' work demands etc. Where the problems are rooted in a lack of technical training a remedy is obvious. Training or other forms of contact between the agency and interviewer may also improve motivation and so reduce conscious malpractice. Various forms of supervision and validation may also improve things.

The problems just discussed can be put down to incompetence rather than wickedness. The borderline between bad practice and cheating is, however, hazy. Fudging on quotas, for example, is certainly a form of cheating. Real cheating is perhaps distinguished by some ambition; the responses to whole parts of the questionnaire are skipped and invented later, whole interviews are concocted or respondent demographics grossly changed to match quota requirements. These practices can be found in all types of field interviewing (or observation) and there are some specialities in qualitative recruitment (see MRS, 1996, for a discussion of good recruitment practice) and especially for group discussions.

At the extreme end of group recruitment malpractice, interviewers and respondents collude, so that the latter misrepresent themselves in terms of recruitment criteria; not so much crude demographics (sex and broad age bands at least, are hard to contrive) but in product usage criteria required to qualify as group members. The incentive for the respondents to do this will be the reward given for attendance (£10 minimum) at something which is hardly hard work and often a pleasant evening out. It is not that hard for a primed respondent to claim to be a user of a particular brand of foodstuff without the group moderator latching on. There is also the problem of 'professional' group goers. Regularly taking part in such research makes the respondent atypical and it is usual practice for the research designer to insist that respondents have not been to another group in, say, six months. The recruiter's job, however, is made easier if she can draw on a tame respondent 'panel' even though they become over-researched. Most experienced qualitative researchers will have eavesdropped on such as 'what are we talking about this week' while waiting for respondents to be brought in.

The problem with cheating of any sort is that it is corrupting. Once done and if not detected, it will be seen as easy and will almost certainly be repeated. What started off as a one-off to solve a pressing problem, becomes standard practice. Agency remedies against cheating include dissuasion through morale building and training, close contact with interviewers, supervision where possible and validation methods to detect it.

The above puts all the blame on interviewers for both bad practice and cheating. But this is hardly fair. Agencies can do much to help their fieldworkers through better training and administration. Furthermore, research designers must shoulder some of the blame. Poor instructions, badly drafted questionnaires, quotas that are virtually impossible to meet, and other design defects, make the interviewer's task that much harder and are no encouragement to good work. Part of the problem is that research executives often have little or no experience of the fieldwork they are ordering. In an ideal world, I would have all trainee research executives serve at least six months as interviewers.

So far I have considered only field rather than phone data collection. Phone research is almost wholly carried out at central locations; in phone rooms with anything up to 100 work stations and equipped with a networked phone system and now often CATI (computer assisted telephone interviewing) terminals. The fact that interviewers are together in one place means that in various ways it is easier to control both variability and cheating. Gross cheating is actually much less likely even without very active steps to prevent it. Assuming some sort of supervision, the interviewer has to at least appear to be interviewing and it is usually as easy to do the work as make it up. Phone systems can also usually allow 'real time' monitoring; a supervisor can listen in silently (unknown to the interviewer)* to the interview and check how the questionnaire is administered, respondent qualification etc. Monitoring can be still closer with CATI; the responses entered can be seen (on the supervisor's terminal) while the interview is overheard. Training can also be carried out more frequently and at lower cost than for field interviewers and every project can be briefed adequately, with problems solved as they arise. Morale is also often stronger because interviewers work together and at the agency; their pay and conditions may be no better than outside interviewers (like them they are typically employed by the hour) but with only a modest management effort they can develop good team loyalty and commitment to the company. Unlike field interviewers, they also often work for one company at a time and perhaps for long periods (although every phone room has its floaters and drifters). Phone interviewer quality is, therefore, much easier to control and effective measures can be taken by the agency at modest cost (which is less true in the case of field interviewers). However, complacency would be misplaced and phone interviewer variability effects cannot be assumed to be always overcome or even cheating completely barred (see Kiecker and Nelson, 1996).

As well as normal field and phone interviewing, there are some more unusual forms of data collection which have specialised quality concerns. These include the various sorts of observation techniques associated with retail auditing and the increasingly used 'mystery shopping' approach. A twist to the latter is that one school of thought has it that more than limited training actually reduces quality. It is the reactions of 'naive' shoppers which are sought.

A final issue is the effect on quality of the public perception of interviewers. Overall, their objective status has not improved (they are possibly drawn from lower social classes than in the 'pin money' era) and their publicly perceived standing has almost certainly gone down. More and

---

* There are some potential legal or regulatory problems in this, though.

more interviewing is done and this itself makes respondents interviewer-wary. Also, there is the problem of people who are not carrying out real research posing as interviewers; timeshare, double glazing and many other salespeople have been known to use a research guise as an 'opener'. There is no legal remedy against such 'sugging' but at various times the research industry has been concerned. The problem has been recognised for at least 20 years and probably started as soon as there was any awareness of market research as an activity. Even worse, market research is claimed to be sometimes used as a cover for crime and some police force leaflets have warned against the dangers from market researchers along with door-to-door beggars, gold buyers and dodgy tradesmen. Certainly, response rates are falling and this is very much a quality problem because of the inevitable increase in non-response bias.

IQCS TO THE RESCUE

IQCS was created to address some or all of the problems discussed in the previous pages of this chapter. Formed in 1986, it is 10 years old at the time of writing but its origins can be traced back to a forerunner; the Interviewer Card Scheme (ICS), set up, under MRS sponsorship, in 1978. This scheme was intended to deal with quality in general but its primary concern was the standing of interviewers and so that the public could differentiate the genuine interviewer from the 'suggers'. The tangible form of this was an industry-standard interviewer identity card which has since become well established and virtually essential to an interviewer. The ICS, however, did not progress in establishing agreed and validated standards for interviewing and interviewers and by 1986 these had come to be seen as a necessity for the industry. In that year, therefore, ICS was replaced by IQCS which had the primary aim of developing minimum standards and setting up a system for establishing companies' compliance with these standards. These areas were considered to be 'trade' matters and best handled by a new body with a defined legal status,* while questions and problems of interviewer identity were left with the MRS as the professional body for the industry The MRS identity card and a freephone service for phoned respondents has continued and with the support of IQCS.

IQCS is a corporate member organisation and, to join, an agency or user of bought-in fieldwork has to both agree to work to the published minimum standards and be assessed or inspected against these. Only companies which pass this process can become or stay as IQCS members. There are in fact two classes of members; fieldwork members (in 1997

---

* A lack of defined legal structure precipitated a terminal crisis for the ICS.

there are approaching 70 of these) which carry out fieldwork themselves (in this sense, field includes phone); and buyers of fieldwork (nearly 20 in 1997). The latter are mainly research companies without in-house data collection resources, and membership commits them to buy in only from IQCS suppliers. Client buyers have also been encouraged to lend support to the idea of minimum standards, not least by recognising that quality fieldwork is likely to cost more than inadequate interviewing, but be of very much greater value. Day-to-day management of IQCS is the responsibility of a Council, the majority of whom are elected by members but also with representatives of other main research bodies; suppliers (AMSO* and ABMRC), clients (AURA) and the MRS. MRQSA now also has a Council representative. As in all these sorts of bodies, much of all the considerable work is taken on by individuals who squeeze it in, without pay, alongside their 'proper' jobs, although IQCS also has the assistance of a part time, paid administrator.

IQCS has two main functions; defining and revising (in the light of feedback from members) minimum standards and administering an assessment or inspection scheme to establish members' and candidate members' compliance with the standards.

IQCS MINIMUM STANDARDS

IQCS minimum standards are a form of service standard; they define how certain sorts of activities should be carried out and, therefore, have an analogy with product standards such as BSs. They are narrow and focused in scope in that they only cover one part (if a vital part) of the research process; data collection. In practice the scope is even narrower since, despite the full title, the standards are entirely concerned with how interviewers will be managed rather than other aspects of data collection. There are three key parts to the Standard – training, appraisal and validation – and these are linked to a requirement for record keeping and documentation so that compliance with the standard can be established. The essentials covered by the key parts of the standard will be now discussed (the standard itself should be read for the full detail) but a point I shall make right now is that whatever criticisms may be made of the standard or of IQCS as a body (since its inception there has been an 'opposition' to it within the industry), it is hard to argue that interviewers should not be adequately trained, their performance appraised

---

*   IQCS is a condition of membership of AMSO. Of the 70 or so IQCS members, about 40 are also AMSO members and 30 are not.

and their work validated in some way or other. Given the structural problems discussed, a denial of this is a recipe for poor quality.

The training requirements are relevant to all interviewers (field and phone) taken on* by an agency and no interviewer should do any client work without some training organised by the particular agency. The level of training depends on the work to be done by the interviewer and whether or not she or he has any previous experience of market research interviewing with another IQCS company (experience with non-IQCS companies is ignored). Even, however, where the interviewer has long and relevant experience with other companies, a minimum level of training must be provided; at least half a day covering the procedures of the agency and to confirm that the individual does have the knowledge claimed. Where such shorter training is given to experienced interviewers, the agency must confirm the past record of the interviewer by contacting the other agency for which he or she has worked. The broad content of the training is specified as is the method of delivery, which must be face to face although it can take place anywhere and be given by a local supervisor as well as head office staff. On completion of 'classroom' training, the new interviewer, whether with prior experience or not, must be accompanied (or monitored in the case of phone unit interviewers) by a supervisor when the first assignment is carried out and no work should be used until this is done.

The general principles of the training programme apply to both phone and field interviewers. However, training of phone interviewers working in one location is much easier to organise and far cheaper than for field interviewers. Phone interviewers have to come into the offices to do their work and the trainer is likely to be a full-time member of the agency's staff. Monitoring during the first assignment is also easily carried out. The training of field interviewers is considerably more expensive; interviewers are generally paid during their training time and the supervisor giving the training certainly expects to be paid. Even if a number of recruits can be trained together (and, therefore, spread the supervisor's cost) initial accompaniment must be one to one. An effect of these requirements is to favour interviewer teams which are used regularly; the cost of training new interviewers for one-off jobs, or who may seldom be needed again, becomes relatively very high, but the alternative of not training at all is hardly a basis for quality. IQCS field training, therefore, has some in-built economies of scale and relatively favours agencies with a larger work throughput but which keep their fieldforce as small as possible consistent with coping with the work loads (not an easy balance). There are also economies in head office administration but these are not as great; such

---

* When an agency joins IQCS all current interviewers are assumed to be trained.

costs tend to go up in steps. The small agency wishing to offer nation-wide coverage is at some cost disadvantage, although IQCS members do include smaller as well as larger companies.

Expensive or not, the IQCS prescribed training levels, however, are hardly excessive. A complete beginner is scarcely adequately prepared for a career as an interviewer on the basis of two days training plus accompaniment. The half day for experienced interviewers may be more debatable (company procedures can be communicated in writing) although the element of testing skills needs to be covered in some way.

The second part of IQCS standards – appraisal – can be regarded as a continuation of initial training. The latter may be deemed adequate for the interviewer to start working but what is to ensure that he or she does not forget what was taught or does not slip into generally bad ways? Field work, at least, is carried out without any direct and ongoing supervision. Frequency and methods of appraisal are specified in IQCS standards. As a minimum, every field interviewer must be appraised once a year and this must include an element of accompaniment during interviews. Field interviewers working frequently must be appraised at least twice a year although one of these appraisals need not include accompaniment during actual work or any face to face contact. Like training, appraisal has economies of scale with the appraisal costs per working day or interview declining with the amount of work carried out by the field interviewer (though there is a step at the point at which two appraisals become necessary). Appraisal is also required for phone unit interviewers, although in practice this presents few problems or additional costs.

As with training, it is hard to argue that the appraisal requirements are any more than necessary to give some confidence that the interviewer is up to the job and help to reduce interviewer variability. It is not, however, any safeguard against outright cheating. Interviewers will hardly misbehave when a supervisor is with them. Safeguards against malpractice, therefore, largely depend on the third part of IQCS standards; validation.

Validation is principally about checking interviewers' work directly with the respondents concerned. In phone units this can be done by monitoring; listening-in without either interviewer or respondent knowing that this has been done. Such validation would certainly catch cheating but, as argued, this is unlikely to be a major problem in a phone room. Phone monitoring is, however, an effective method of establishing levels of interviewer variability and reducing it through follow-on training and by feedback to the interviewers.

Phone interviewing validation is, therefore, real time. By contrast field validation is nearly always *post hoc*.* Some time after the questionnaires

---

* Venue based validation including group discussions may approximate to real time.

or other data are returned, the respondent is recontacted (by post, phone or face to face) and a 'back-checking' interview carried out to establish recall of the initial interview and to check some of the responses (eg key demographics or product usage which will be relevant to quota selection or respondent qualification). Of course, recontacted respondents may have forgotten the interview and, therefore, give a seemingly negative result, but a consistent pattern of such results will certainly indicate problems where further action is required. The standard specifies the proportion of interviews completed in a project which must be validated (10 per cent generally for field compared with 5 per cent for phone centre interviews), the methods to be used and content coverage and also requires that each interviewer is systematically selected for validation of their work.

The prescribed validation of field interviewing provides some safeguards against cheating; the interviewer who consistently makes up questionnaires is likely to be caught out when recontact is attempted with imaginary respondents. Similarly, back-checking may identify some less extreme malpractice such as gross quota fiddling. It is hardly, however, a method of establishing or minimising interviewer variability; *post hoc* recontact is just not sensitive enough to achieve this. However, the prescribed levels and selection of interviews for back-checking appear implicitly to assume that validation is a form of process control rather than the detection of fraud.

Another approach to validation is the checking of completed questionnaires. This can identify problems which need correcting through retraining (eg adequacy of recording open-ended responses, completeness of questionnaires, skip patterns etc) and may even give an indication of fraudulent interviews (inconsistency in the made-up responses). Such 'editing' can involve inspection of paper questionnaires (all or a sample) or by running various validation tests of data once they are entered on to computer files. CAPI or CATI interviews arguably need less validation of this sort since with automatic routeing etc there is less chance of making errors (and automatic recording of times of interview makes cheating harder or less attractive). However, in this case as well, some post data entry validation can be usefully carried out. IQCS standards, however, only briefly cover the editing of paper questionnaires and as 'good practice' rather than as a mandatory requirement. Validation of fieldwork through feedback from data analysis is not covered at all; this is outside the 'field' domain.

The above summarises the requirements of the three key parts of the standard. In addition there are important requirements for adequate record keeping and documentation. These enable the agency to control fieldwork quality management and in addition are the means by which IQCS, through its team of inspectors, establishes member or candidate member compliance with the standards. Which records must be kept are specified but the general principles are that project records have to show which interviewers worked on the job, what they did and what validation was carried out. In addition interviewer files must be maintained to show the training and appraisal records of interviewers, the work they have been assigned, the outcome of validation of their work and various administrative details. Keeping such records requires a significant clerical input. Computerised records can aid efficiency and facilitate more comprehensive auditing of compliance with the standards. The standards also specify documentation that must be given to interviewers including training manuals and an annually issued MRS identity card. What is not specified in IQCS is any need for formal quality assurance; systems to assist agencies in ensuring consistent compliance with the standard. There is no requirement to have written procedures covering how the standards are to be implemented in the particular company.

IQCS standards also cover other areas which I have chosen not to discuss at all. The most important of these are the requirements concerning field based supervisors. It is they who largely recruit, train and appraise interviewers.

ASSESSMENT AND INSPECTION

From inception, IQCS has required its members to be inspected to establish that they do comply with the standards. Membership of IQCS is, therefore, more than mere good intentions. It is a commitment to what is, in effect, third-party assessment.

Inspections are carried out by a small team employed, part time, by IQCS. The individuals concerned all have practical and long experience of market research fieldwork. Inspections are carried out when a company applies to join the scheme and, thereafter, annually. The inspection work takes place at the agency's office with the time spent linked to the size of the company (effectively a minimum of one day) and very largely consists of checking records with cross referencing of project and interviewer files. This establishes whether training, appraisals and validation have been carried out to the standards, although, strictly speaking, the inspection only proves that records exist indicating that the requirements have been met. There is, therefore, some potential for the companies to cheat through false recording but this probably happens to only a minor extent. It is hard to imagine that a company would go to all the trouble involved without having a basic willingness to comply. IQCS has been criticised because its inspection is very largely concerned with historical records rather than directly establishing fieldwork competence.

Realistically, however, it is hard to envisage how any inspection or assessment, at a realistic cost, can be other than largely record based. It should also be said that inspections are no walk-over. Candidate companies sometimes fail, as do, occasionally, existing members.

The award of the annual membership certificate follows inspection and is made by IQCS Council on the recommendation (but not the decision) of its inspectors.

Inspection of course has a cost to the companies. For a smaller company the minimum annual fees are around £500 going up to around £2000 for the largest member. User members pay less. The inspection fees, however, are the minor part of the total costs of complying with the standard. Training, appraisal, validation and the maintenance of records all have substantial internal costs and, as indicated, the basis of these relatively favour larger rather than smaller companies. However, arguably, these should be seen as the price that must be paid for maintaining levels of data collection quality consistent with meeting clients' needs rather than as just IQCS costs.

IS IT ALL ENOUGH?

One point to make immediately in considering whether IQCS standards are adequate is that they must be acceptable, taking into account the costs entailed, to the companies required to implement them. It is easy to think up more and more quality hurdles, but unless members are willing to follow them they will vote with their feet, and leave the scheme. Similarly there is no point in being critical because IQCS standards do not address the full scope of data collection. This is not the intention; only the work of interviewers is addressed and not the important contribution of design work (a bad questionnaire will fail to produce valid data regardless of the interviewers) or the project management of fieldwork.

In relation to ensuring that interviewers are trained and for ongoing appraisal, the requirements of IQCS, are, in my opinion, the minimum that can be regarded as acceptable. Quality agencies should aim higher. An effect of these requirements is to impose uneconomic burden on some smaller companies – those offering nationwide field interviewing but with low work throughputs. However, this is a business viability rather than a quality problem and it is hardly satisfactory to argue that such operations should be excused from working to minimally acceptable standards just because it is uneconomic. In other businesses, if the minimum quality level cannot be met or it is not offered at all, the operators fade out. The principle seems fair enough in market research as well. I am not suggesting, however, that non-members of IQCS should be banned from trading.

Some may well meet or surpass the minimum standards even though they choose not to be members of the scheme. Furthermore, small operations can provide fieldwork to the standards and not be at a serious cost disadvantage if they are selective; phone units have less economies of scale in some respects and field operations can provide selective services such as group recruitment or not attempt full national coverage. They can also buy in their research and many companies, large as well as small, choose to do this.

This leaves the question of validation and here I regard the standards as more problematical. Validation suggests a form of process control which in this application concerns seeking to minimise interviewer variability. The standards are loosely based on quality control through sampling, to meet the specified back-checking or monitoring levels. In the case of phone unit interviewing, monitoring does offer an effective quality control tool. The interviewer's work can be monitored in real time and without his or her knowledge (to ensure that the performance is not a special effort) and instant feedback and training can be given. In the case of field, however, it is very doubtful that back-checking provides any real validation in terms of process control. It is just too crude, relying as it does on *post hoc* methods. Instead, minimising interviewer variability must depend on adequate training (the existing requirements are arguably not enough in this respect) and appraisal. Editing validation in its various forms also offers some means of establishing and controlling variability. It is surprising that editing is only a good practice recommendation and that the standards make no reference to data analysis feedback.

Back-checking is a reasonably effective control on outright cheating with the deterrent effect* as important as the actual detection of malpractice. However, training, appraisal, general communication and morale building can all have a useful role in the prevention of cheating as well and perhaps this should be made explicit in the standards. There is also a need to examine the levels of back-checking specified. What is special about 10 per cent or 5 per cent? Are these levels enough or too high? There is a partial assumption that this form of validation should be random – as are methods used in manufacturing process control. But if back-checking is really about detecting fraud, perhaps the approach should be in concentrating efforts where problems are most likely. This is the practice in other areas of business – eg the work of financial auditors, tax inspectors etc – but the IQCS standards only partly introduce this concept and rather half heartedly at that. There is, therefore, a need to re-examine validation of at least field interviewing. Even in relation to fraud, complacency is not justified.

---

* This is why it may appear that higher levels of back-checking lead to less detected fraud; bad interviewers know that the chances of getting caught are greater.

Any consideration of whether IQCS is enough should include the role of the inspectors. Undoubtably they all do a good job but they are not fully trained as assessors and are not exposed to the stimulus of taking a wider view of organisations or even aspects of market research not within the field or phone departments. However, it is possible that inspection of compliance with field standards will in the future change for reasons to be discussed in the next chapter.

These then are my views of the adequacy of IQCS standards. I am conscious that I have not really considered the question of whether having industry standards and assessment arrangements is desirable and necessary at all. However, this question is better discussed in the broader context of industry standards across the whole research process and this is the subject of the next chapter.

9

Standards for the whole research process – MRQSA

The last chapter discussed some of the quality problems of data collection and how a market research industry service standard – IQCS – was developed to help overcome these. More recently, corresponding standards have been prepared by the Market Research Quality Standards Association (MRQSA) for the whole research process.

MRQSA ORIGINS

Although MRQSA is a natural development from IQCS – extending minimum standards from just one to all research processes – its origins and the catalyst to its birth lay elsewhere; in ISO 9000 (or BS 5750 as it was at the time).

In the early 1990s, one or two research companies, for whatever reasons, decided to implement and be assessed to BS 5750. Having achieved this, the pioneers, being good marketing companies, were not shy of their own success and claimed or implied that certification to BS 5750 indicated their commitment to a high quality of research. Such claims and the generally high profile of BS 5750 at the time, led to a quite fierce debate in the market research industry about quality in general and the relevance or otherwise of general as well as industry-specific standards. Much that was said at the time was ill-informed and particularly in relation to BS 5750 which was widely misunderstood, including by people who should have known better. These included some heads of larger research companies who at the time publicly castigated BS 5750 as of no value whatsoever and totally irrelevant to their own companies. Significantly, in the four or five years since this time, these same companies have nearly all now implemented BS 5750/ISO 9000. Leaving aside petty jealousies and politicking, the main substance of the case against BS 5750 was that it did not prove that a company had achieved high quality levels in its research services. On the contrary, it was said that an agency could work well below any sort of acceptable professional standards but still be able to gain BS 5750.

The argument that BS 5750 did not indicate the achievement of any particular level of quality was of course completely true, but it was hardly a valid criticism of the standard. As described in Chapter 7, BS 5750/ISO 9000 is a standard for managing quality and for quality assurance and it is not a service or product standard. It is a standard of capability; the capability to meet defined standards, whatever these are, consistently and constantly. What the defined standards should be cannot be found within the Standard but must come from elsewhere. Therefore, to criticise BS 5750 for not defining minimum standards for market research is analogous to damning a football team for being hopeless at cricket. Much of the debate was a futile tilting at imaginary windmills. Of course the early uptakers of BS 5750 were not wholly blameless either. Even though they understood what the Standard truly meant, they were content to let others take their certification as somehow indicating superior quality levels.

Eventually, things calmed down and a broad consensus about quality emerged. This was that while companies did need to manage their quality and BS 5750 might be an effective tool to achieve this, the market research industry now needed some defined minimum quality levels to which reputable research suppliers should work. It was also accepted that there was a need for some form of third-party assessment to make such standards enforceable and to enable agencies to demonstrate compliance. IQCS was of course a model for this, but the scope of any new standards needed to include the whole research process and not just data collection. Various ways of developing and formulating new standards were discussed and explored, including a British Standard for market research services, somehow modifying BS 5750 to make it specific to the research industry and having independent industry standards on the model of IQCS.

The British Standard option was pursued seriously for a time with meetings between senior research people and the BSI. The attraction was to have standards embodied in an 'official' document and one which would have a standing among those not in the research industry (to whom, by contrast, the industry's own standards might mean little). However, the barriers to achieve this proved to be insurmountable in the short term. There were no existing BSs covering services rather than physical product and BSI did not appear to be ready to support the development of such standards at the time. Also, it was clear that the timescale for develop-ment of official BSs would be far longer than seemed desirable; the research industry was used to moving comparatively quickly. Therefore, it was decided that the BS route was not a practical one to take at the time although, as will be mentioned later, events have come near to full circle, with a BS now a likelihood. One other outcome of discussions with BSI, was the recognition of the need for any service standards to not only have wide support but to be seen to have this in a formal way. BSI had indicated that any long-term progress to a BS necessitated this. In any case this would be politically desirable within the industry.

The option of developing an industry-specific BS 5750 had some attrac-tions. The concept was to take this standard as a framework and add in some specific service standard requirements. Within the heading covering inspection and testing, for example, some specific types of inspection or tests might be added. After little discussion, however, this option was clearly a non-starter. The official standard, applicable to all businesses and with a comparable international standard could not be revised or reissued just to suit the needs of one small industry. Moreover, even if some sort of hybrid BS 5750 could be developed and offered as a standard against which to be assessed there would be no way of forcing market research companies to be assessed against the hybrid rather than the 'official' BS 5750 and the result could be more rather than less confusion about standards and what they all meant. There were also some political problems with a BS 5750 based approach; the debate about the value of BS 5750 had generated con-siderable heat and some were against it in any guise.

The option left, therefore, was for the market research industry to develop standards of its own covering the whole research process. With the need for industry-wide support to be not only present but demon-strable, it was decided that the best approach would be to set up a new representative body with the responsibility of both developing the new standards and of arranging an effective means of third-party assessment. MRQSA was the resulting body with a corporate membership repre-senting all other trade and professional bodies within market research; the two supplier associations (AMSO and ABMRC), users of research (AURA and ISBA) and the professional body and two interest groups (MRS, AQRP and SRA). Finally IQCS was also represented; from the start there was no wish to have the new body appear to be a competitor to IQCS.

MRQSA was officially constituted in late 1994 with a Council of management representing each member body. By January 1996 a first version of its standards – the Service Standard for Market Research – was published, now replaced with a 1997 updated version (see MRQSA 1997), and with arrangements in place to offer independent third-party assessment. By the end of 1996 a few research companies had been successfully assessed and awarded an MRQSA certificate.

SCOPE AND NATURE OF MRQSA STANDARDS

The new standards were developed to cover the whole of the research process. This did not and could not practically mean that every possible activity undertaken in market research was covered or referred to in the standards. What is meant by covering the whole research process is that, in terms of *ad hoc* research, the standards apply from initial discussion of a project, through proposal writing and commission to the main steps of doing the work up and to reporting to the client. Continuous research projects are also fully covered; for the most part the steps in *ad hoc* research correspond to those in continuous research but without a defined finish point. The new standards are for suppliers of research services to implement rather than buyers or users, although the latter through their own organisations – AURA and ISBA – support MRQSA. In-house research departments, acting as internal agencies to other parts of their organisations, however, can certainly also consider implementing the standards.

For ease of drafting and understanding, the service standards are broken into three main modules; managing the executive elements of research, data collection and data processing. As will be discussed more fully, the data collection standards were not in fact drafted anew by MRQSA; the IQCS minimum standards were simply imported in their entirety. There are also two other important parts to the Standard; quality assurance and arrangements for assessment. Each module and part to the MRQSA standards is discussed in some detail but a preliminary issue to consider is the general nature of the standards; what sort of activities are they designed to cover and legislate for? Before describing what these are, it is useful to define them negatively – what is not attempted in the standards.

By and large what is not covered is any attempt to define what is a right and valid research design. When and where qualitative rather than quantitative research should be used, sampling and questionnaire design principles, on what basis and how data can be generalised and how inferences are drawn, are all examples of what is not covered in the standards. These all touch on issues of quality as excellence rather than relative quality and meeting specifications. It is not of course that these areas are considered unimportant to quality in research. On the contrary, the view is that these are fundamental matters and if anything too important to be dealt with within MRQSA type standards. Instead issues of what constitutes 'right' research are left as professional matters to be defined by an informal consensus. It is argued that at the leading edge of research practice there may be debate and dissension on what is 'right' but that, nevertheless, there is a large body of research practice which is reasonably certain, accepted and understood by all practitioners of any experience.

I dispute that this view of professional 'standards' (put in quotation marks because they are not standards) is completely valid, even if it is pragmatically acceptable. The reason that MRQSA could not sensibly define right methods is because of a certain lack of consensus on what is right. This in turn reflects both some of the shifting intellectual ground on which market research is built and that market research is still a very open profession. Any attempt to define right research, in simple statements, would inevitably have been criticised by people who could reasonably claim authority within the industry. Whatever else, MRQSA requires wide consensus which would have been impossible to achieve for standards of this nature.

There are, therefore, good practical reasons for the course taken but it should be noted that in other knowledge businesses, 'right' methods are defined and set as standards. Accountancy is the best known example. It may be that there can be legitimate debate on how goodwill should be treated in accounting statements, but this has not prevented the responsible body from setting standards and, moreover, standards, along with all the other accounting standards, which have virtually the force of law. However, accountancy is not market research. Probably researchers would contend that although some aspects of accountancy might be sophisticated and require extensive knowledge because it deals with normative knowledge, it is all a lot surer and more certain than what is appropriate in researching markets and consumers. No doubt accountants would not wholly concur to this view. However, the fact remains that standardising 'right practice' in market research has not proved to be practical as yet and is unlikely to be so in the foreseeable future.

Returning then to what MRQSA standards do seek to encompass, these can be listed under three broad headings which apply across all three modules:

- Meeting requirements.
- The execution of a research design.
- The services supplied to a client over and above 'right' research practice.

In several parts, the standards are concerned with establishing the client's requirements from research and practical steps to ensure these are met in practice. The ultimate client is of course of primary concern, but the standard recognises that day to day, many people working on projects,

155

will have closer contact with staff in other departments and they can be usefully regarded as internal clients.

While the standards do not seek to address what is 'right' research design, they do cover how the design is put into practice, with various controls and checks specified to increase the likelihood that what is intended in the design happens in practice (and at the first attempt).

Client services cover things such as keeping clients informed of progress and of any problems arising, timeliness, involving them where appropriate in decisions (eg questionnaire approval), how the 'product' – reports etc – should be delivered and the back-up that clients should expect, eg in terms of records retention. Arguably these, and for that matter the execution of the research design, can all be considered aspects of meeting requirements.

This then is the general nature of the standards. I shall now consider the contents of the specific modules and parts of the published standard in the order in which they are set out in the document.

QUALITY ASSURANCE

Since MRQSA was born out of the perceived limitations of BS 5750/ISO 9000 – a standard for quality assurance – it may seem odd that the first substantial section of the published standards is devoted to quality assurance. However, the need for companies to ensure that the standards are effectively put into practice had been accepted from the start. In this respect it was intended that MRQSA should overcome a weakness of IQCS; a lack of any requirement for internal quality assurance methods.

For the first year or so while the standards were being developed, it had been assumed by most members of MRQSA Council that the anticipated assessment route would require companies to have a quality system to ISO 9000 in place and certificated (by this time BS 5750 had been dropped from the nomenclature of the standard). Again, however, politics influenced the decisions. The need for consensus was built into MRQSA and the significant level of opposition to ISO 9000 meant that a formal requirement for certification to this standard was not an option that could be pursued; at least in 1995. The agreed compromise was that MRQSA should define its own quality assurance model, incorporating the framework and a good part of the contents of ISO 9000, but in a rather looser and less bureaucratic way and it was this approach which was eventually incorporated into the standard.

The MRQSA quality assurance requirements or model overlap with all but four of the 20 main headings of ISO 9001. The four ISO 9001 headings not reflected in the MRQSA model are: control of inspection;

measuring and test equipment; servicing; statistical techniques and internal quality audits. The first three have but limited application in market research (see Chapter 7). Internal quality audits are another matter. Any company implementing formal standards will inevitably need to check whether what is intended is actually achieved and internal auditing is basically no more than this. However, leaving out any formal requirement of the sort from the MRQSA quality assurance model means that companies need not impose on themselves the full rigour of formal auditing as specified in ISO 9000 and can carry out any checking of effectiveness in a more relaxed and less demanding way. This may well suit at least smaller companies.

The other 16 main headings of ISO 9001 are covered in the MRQSA model but in many cases with rather less specified, mandatory detail and in a more flexible way. The need for management responsibility is an example of this. However, despite differences in wording, other headings of ISO 9000 are fully covered by the MRQSA model and, when it comes to implementing it, the MRQSA model has some 70 per cent to 80 per cent of what is needed to meet ISO 9000. Once a company has developed a system to meet the MRQSA quality assurance model, the extra step up to ISO 9000 is not that very great.

In practical application, the quality assurance requirements of the MRQSA model, or for that matter ISO 9000, concern having effective procedures in place which define what needs to be done as a minimum to offer clients a quality service. The requirements set out in the other parts of the MRQSA standard also need to be brought into the quality system.

What, though, of those companies which already have ISO 9000 or wish to have it alongside the MRQSA standards; perhaps because they believe certification to an established, general and international standard is well worth having? While some of the requirements of ISO 9000 are not covered by the MRQSA model, it is a different matter the other way round; everything in the MRQSA quality assurance model is certainly covered by ISO 9000 (and more so). It therefore follows that a company meeting the ISO 9001 or ISO 9002 models also meet the MRQSA model and this has been taken into account in the assessment arrangements. A company with an ISO 9000 system already in place is also at a practical advantage when it comes to incorporating the other requirements of MRQSA standards into the documented system. The framework to do this will already be in place.

To avoid possible confusion, I will stress again that quality assurance models in general concern the application of quality standards and do not define what these are and in this the MRQSA model is no different to ISO 9000. It is in the rest of the standard where the quality standards are defined. It is the purpose of the methods set out in the quality assurance part to ensure consistent and constant adherence to these standards. No further detail about the quality assurance is attempted here since it is better to read the Standard itself. To illustrate the range of the quality assurance model, however, the subheadings are as follows. The numbers in brackets and italics are cross references to ISO 9001 clause numbering* (see Chapter 7).

MRQSA quality assurance headings

- 2.0 The need for quality assurance (*4.1*)
- 2.1 Quality assurance procedures (*4.2, 4.5*)
- 2.2 Client contracts (*4.3*)
- 2.3 Planning, controlling and checking research activities (*4.4, 4.9, 4.10, 4.12*)
- 2.4 Purchasing (*4.6*)
- 2.5 Staff training (*4.18*)
- 2.6 Dealing with problems (*4.13, 4.14*)
- 2.7 Keeping and safeguarding records and materials (*4.7, 4.8, 4.15, 4.16*)

MANAGING THE EXECUTIVE ELEMENTS OF RESEARCH

Having standards concerning how the executive part of research should be carried out is a new departure and was potentially controversial. The fact that in the event there has been little negative reaction reflects that MRQSA sought the broadest possible consensus and that what is included is, for the most part, already well established good practice in many agencies – in general, the standards were meant to reflect existing good practice.

The scope of this module of the standards covers the tasks typically carried out by a research executive, including research design and proposal writing, questionnaire development, briefing of interviewers and reporting as well as overall project management and liaison with the client. However, the 'executive' can go by any title and the standards allow for more than one person to have executive responsibility for a project. There is, therefore, sufficient flexibility to fit any organisational structure for both

---

* However, it should not be assumed because an MRQSA heading cross-references to an ISO 9001 clause that the full requirements of the latter are met; the ISO 9001 clauses may be and in many cases are fuller and more demanding.

ad hoc and continuous research. At some critical stages in the process – the overall research design and questionnaire development – 'review' is required; independent checking of the executive's work. Depending, however, on the size and structure of an agency, it may be practically difficult to have another person review the work of the first executive – quite possibly no one else is sufficiently knowledgeable – and the standards leave considerable flexibility in this respect. The client's acceptance of a proposal, for example, is considered to be a form of review. While this may be a practical solution to an organisational problem, it is arguably less of a quality solution.

The executive module is prescriptive about what has to be done at various points in the process. Some of the contents of quotations and proposals are defined (proposals are assumed to have a research design element while quotations are responses to a tight specification). Minimal levels of client contact and liaison, including through a client participation schedule, are specified as is the need for ensuring the adequate briefing of the interviewing team and the data processing department. At the reporting stage, the minimum details of the research methodology which must be given to the client are defined; these appear quite onerous and appear to go to a level of detail which many clients may not wish to know. However, arguably, professional work should be transparent in this way and in any case the standards require in this respect no more than is in the MRS Code of Conduct.* The difference is that, unlike observance of the Code, adherence to MRQSA standards is validated if a company chooses to be assessed.

The executive standards also cover the storage and safeguarding of project records (again generally no more than set out in the MRS code) and looking after materials supplied by clients such as test products, visuals for prompts and information of all sorts. Finally the executive module specifies checking at various points in the process, including tabulations and the final report and, in qualitative work, of respondent recruitment. The review concept has already been mentioned and this too is a form of checking.

The requirements of the executive standard fit into the quality assurance framework, either as per the MRQSA model or ISO 9000. In terms of the latter, the standards specified relate mainly to contract review, design and process control and inspection and test status.

As I mentioned at the beginning of this section, there is little that is controversial in the executive standards because for the most part no more than the codification of common practice is attempted. Arguably,

---

*   The standards as a whole require that executives act within the code in all respects and ensure that other staff involved do so as well.

therefore, the requirements are quite low. However, they do provide a standard against which conformance can be established and, therefore, potentially a means of differentiating those companies which publicly adhere to minimum acceptable standards from those which do not. Any company is of course free to exceed the standards and over time they may become more extensive and tougher. The minimum can always be raised if the consensus to do so exists.

DATA COLLECTION

The data collection module is the longest in MRQSA standards but none of it was drafted by MRQSA. Instead, the already well established IQCS standards were simply incorporated without any substantial amendment at all. Furthermore, for the foreseeable future, MRQSA will continue to leave the responsibility for the data collection standards to IQCS and the two bodies will work closely together to ensure full compatibility in both standards and assessment arrangements. The practical implication for a company which is already a member of IQCS is that they already work to the data collection standards required by MRQSA and the only change which might be required in this area is to develop documented procedures which incorporate the data collection standards.

DATA PROCESSING

The third module of the MRQSA standards has proved to be the most controversial, more so than the executive module. In part, this is because the practices covered vary quite widely through the market research industry. Also, until now, data processing operations have had only limited exposure to formal service standards. Data processing is clearly a vital link in achieving quality and the work involved includes both routine clerical operations (record editing, coding of open-ended questions and data entry) and more skilled and professional level work (programming and specing and of course more sophisticated statistical analysis of data). At each stage there is potential for error through either simple mistakes or for more fundamental reasons. Coding, for example, although usually regarded as a straightforward clerical task, is quite problematical (see MRS, 1983; Owen, 1991) and may introduce more errors than sampling or even data collection. At the worst, coders misunderstand the inter-viewers' recording of responses and the interviewers themselves may well have misrecorded or misunderstood what the respondent actually said (and this may not reflect what is truly believed).

The new data processing standards cover project management, defining how parts of the process should be carried out and also require checking or verification at various points.

Project management requirements include client liaison and meeting client requirements and internal management of the process. In both respects the data processing standards mirror and restate the executive module.* There are also some 'housekeeping' requirements concerning the safe keeping of records and ensuring each primary record (eg questionnaires) is uniquely identified – essential when tracing back to correct errors or verify operations such as coding or data entry.

Standards for carrying out some of the main steps in data processing are prescribed and these include developing a code frame for open-ended responses, the coding process itself, data entry, managing computer files and the presentation of output including labelling of tables and electronic files. Although the main emphasis is on the processing of traditional paper records, data from CATI and CAPI are also included, if rather sketchily.

Inspection or verification is specified at various points, including the editing of records, preparation of code frames, coding itself, data entry, data file editing and the final output. Second person verification is specified at most of these stages and, in coding and data entry, minimum levels of verification are required. This in particular has proved to be controversial. A not wholly resolved aspect of verification is whether the purpose is to identify any errors which arise out of the nature of the job (eg data entry mistakes because of questionnaire layout) or because of deficiencies in people (eg a data entry operator is simply inaccurate). In developing verification methods and levels, these rather different purposes which verification is meant to achieve were, arguably, not adequately distinguished.

The data processing standards have also been criticised for giving only scant attention to CATI, CAPI or automatic data entry through such as optical readers. Yet use of such technologies has a fundamental impact on data processing. Data entry as such, at the processing stage, for example, is obviated with CATI and CAPI. However, the use of computers in the interviewing process only transfers data entry to an earlier point in the process; the interviewer acts as the data entry clerk but any problems of this are not recognised anywhere in the standards. CATI and CAPI are also arguably given insufficient attention in the other modules of MRQSA standards. The use of these techniques will undoubtedly continue to grow

---

* This problem and the inclusion of CATI and CAPI have been addressed in the later 1997 standards.

in importance and there may need to be a greater emphasis, in the standards generally, on these methods.

ASSESSMENT

From inception, MRQSA's aims included putting in place a means by which companies could be independently assessed to the standards. One possible means of achieving this would have been for MRQSA to set up its own team of inspectors and follow the IQCS model. However, this approach was rejected at an early stage. Purely practical problems were one reason since MRQSA had (and has) no full-time administrative staff. Also, it was considered that assessment ought to be carried out by bodies recognised in the wider business world since this might carry more credibility than a purely 'private' industry scheme. Finally, although it was agreed that ISO 9000 should not be a precondition of MRQSA assessment, it was recognised that some companies would certainly wish to be assessed for both MRQSA and ISO 9000 (several already had ISO 9000 certification) and to minimise costs they would want to combine the two in some way. The assessment arrangements that were agreed by MRQSA Council and set out in the standards' document, fully took account of these concerns.

Assessment to MRQSA standards is carried out by approved (by MRQSA) independent bodies each of which is also accredited by UKAS to carry out assessment of market research companies to ISO 9000. At the time of writing four such bodies are on the MRQSA approved list (see list at the end of this chapter). Companies can request any of these bodies to assess them for either MRQSA alone or MRQSA in combination with ISO 9000. MRQSA has liaised closely with the bodies to agree how the MRQSA element of the assessment should be conducted and reported but has no involvement in how ISO 9000 assessment should be conducted (this is done to the standards specified and monitored by UKAS).

The assessment process for MRQSA mirrors ISO 9000. During the initial assessment all parts of a company and all relevant parts of the standard are covered. The work involved includes both checking the quality system documentation to ensure the requirements of the standards are fully met and documented and then establishing whether the system is actually followed in practice. The length of time involved in this initial assessment depends very much on the size of the company concerned but is unlikely to involve less than a full day's work by the assessment body's staff. A greater input will be involved for larger companies. Where ISO 9000 and MRQSA assessment are combined, the actual work undertaken by the assessor is not likely to be significantly different to a MRQSA-alone assessment. In either case the same quality system is assessed. If, on the basis of their findings, the assessment body feels able to recommend that the company should be given the MRQSA certificate, a short report is forwarded to MRQSA Council which is then responsible for issuing a certificate. Formally, the decision to do this rests with MRQSA alone but in practice Council is unlikely to reject a positive recommendation by an approved assessment body.

After initial assessment there is a requirement for continuous follow-up assessment. The normal practice in this respect is for the assessment body to make a surveillance visit every six months and on each occasion to cover part of the company and part of the standards but with complete coverage achieved over a two-year cycle. After each surveillance visit the assessment body completes a report for MRQSA with a recommendation (if justified) that the company remain certificated (MRQSA retains the right to withdraw its certificate if the findings from continuous assessment are not satisfactory). Again, the MRQSA continuous assessment process is modelled on ISO 9000 and the two can be combined.

Assessment has a cost, of course. Assessment bodies charge companies for their services and the rates for both initial and continuous assessment are as much as for ISO 9000. The differences in cost of MRQSA alone and ISO 9000 combined assessments are only marginal. In addition MRQSA itself levies an administration charge for processing the assessment and award of certificates.

Assessment to MRQSA is against the current version of the standards and against all sections which apply to the work of the company being assessed. All companies are required to meet the quality assurance requirements of the MRQSA standard and assessment of this part is either by the assessment body against the MRQSA quality assurance model or by prior or concurrent assessment to ISO 9001 or 9002. All companies are also required to be assessed against the executive module, regardless of whether they are a full service agency or not. It is assumed that even a purely field and tab operation will necessitate some 'executive' involvement. The data collection and data processing modules, however, are only relevant where these processes are carried out in-house, although there are some restrictions on buying in these services (with a presumption that, where possible, the services should be bought from MRQSA assessed suppliers). A further complication is that for data processing, MRQSA recognises current membership of IQCS (and, therefore, inspection by IQCS) as adequate evidence of compliance with this module of the standards. This means that, in practice, an assessment body may not audit data collection if the company can produce a current IQCS certificate. It is anticipated, however, that this arrangement will be for a transitionary period only and that in the longer run companies will choose assessment of all operations together including data collection. This will be cheaper than having a separate IQCS inspection as well and in the longer run it is possible that separate IQCS inspection will fade away.

IMPLEMENTATION

Implementation of MRQSA is no different in principle (or largely in practice) to ISO 9000. In either case the company needs to develop a unique quality system which both matches the requirements of the standard and the particular needs and structure of the business. Once the system is designed, it is then a matter of getting the company and its staff to work to the system. When the system is working, assessment can be arranged. There is a requirement that the system must have been operating for at least three months before assessment, although in practice the elapsed period is likely to be longer.

A company can choose to implement purely the MRQSA Standard including the MRQSA quality assurance model or both ISO 9001 or 9002 and MRQSA. The extra demands for the latter course are not major and particularly if some form of internal quality auditing is carried out. As already mentioned, internal auditing is not specifically required by the MRQSA quality assurance model but, in practice, successful implementation requires this process in some form.

Chapter 12 discusses implementation of effective systems in more detail.

THE FUTURE OF MRQSA

At the time of writing it is too early to be sure that MRQSA will prove to be successful in terms of take-up. However, the signs are positive and it seems very probable that it will become an established part of the market research industry.

The standards themselves are not immutable and, on the contrary, it is expected that they will be revised from time to time, and some were made in the first 1997 revision. As with the original draft, it is MRQSA Council's responsibility to make revisions, but they will only do so after inviting as wide comment as possible and seeking a high level of consensus. As more companies are assessed to the standard it is possible that responsibility for revisions will be handed over to them (as per IQCS).

Before MRQSA was constituted, the possibility of setting market research service standards as a British Standard had been considered but rejected. However, this option is now being pursued with the support of

BSI. However, now it is a case of adapting an existing standard and formatting it as a BS rather than starting afresh. The interest in doing this links to the potential for a European or international market research standard. This aspect will be discussed in Chapter 11.

WHAT HAS MRQSA ACHIEVED?

Another way of asking the question is, why is a service standard for market research needed at all? The case for MRQSA includes the effect on raising standards, providing reassurance to clients and a flatter playing-field for suppliers.

By defining the minimum service levels that any market research company should provide to its clients, widely accepted service standards should at least help prevent grossly substandard services; both buyers and suppliers should know the minimum that ought to be expected. Assessment to the standards also means that commitment is demonstrable and not just a matter of good intentions. This is in contrast to such as the MRS code where there is no real mechanism for ensuring adherence and only the most flagrant and public breaches are ever likely to be brought out into the open. A more uncertain question is, however, whether defining minimum standards – and that is all MRQSA aims to do – encourages agencies to surpass these or just meet them. Theoretical arguments can be advanced in either case and eventually the matter needs judging empirically, but it is still far to early too do this.

MRQSA standards provide reassurance to buyers and users of research; they can assume that an assessed supplier works to a minimally acceptable level and in many areas which would not normally be transparent – in many aspects of the research process, there is no way a research buyer can directly establish whether the project work has been done to acceptable standards. Independent assessment will provide some comfort. There is of course no guarantee that an MRQSA certificated company will do a brilliant job of work, but the chances of it being really bad are probably significantly less. In time, therefore, buyers may come to see MRQSA assessment as a necessary pre-condition for inviting quotations from a company or at least as a strongly positive factor. But other considerations will of course still apply, including the details of the proposal put forward, prior experience of the agency, its general reputation and of course price.

Linked to this is that agencies working to the same minimum standards will be competing in a more comparable way. Research prices can always be brought down if corners are cut, but with companies working to the same minimum standards, clients are protected from suppliers tempted to win business on the basis of offering research which seems to meet the need but is in fact deficient. Companies implementing MRQSA, will certainly incur costs, as do those which are members of IQCS, and they will wish buyers of research to be able to distinguish suppliers of this standard from others which may offer lower prices. If quality is compromised, lower prices do not mean better value. Poor research is never a bargain.

Finally, MRQSA should help enhance the status of the market research industry in the UK. A public and visible commitment to minimum standards should help raise the profile and make research better respected and in greater demand by decision makers in this country and worldwide. Obviously this is to the benefit of everyone working in the profession, whether as suppliers or users.

MRQSA APPROVED ASSESSMENT BODIES

- BSI Quality Assurance – PO Box 375, Milton Keynes MK1 6LL. Tel: 01908 220908.
- MQA – The Brackens, London Road, Ascot, Berkshire SL5 8BG. Tel: 01344 882400.
- PECS – Resource House, 144 High Street, Rayleigh, Essex SS6 7BO. Tel: 01268 770135.
- SGS Yarsley ICS – Formal House, Oldmixon Crescent, Weston Super Mare, Somerset BS24 9AL. Tel: 01934 641608.

10

People quality – Investors in People

Quality, of whatever sort, depends on people and no more so than in a market research business. Systems and standards can help deliver quality, but not without trained and willing managers and staff. A major need in quality management, therefore, is to ensure staff have the necessary skills and commitment.

WHAT IS REQUIRED?

What is required of staff to deliver quality? There are two major and linked requirements; commitment and skills. Commitment is about accepting the importance of quality and wanting to deliver it, all the time. Various morale building approaches, management leadership, including by example and exhortation, all have their part to play. So does staff involvement in quality improvement through such as quality circles, special task groups and involvement in the problem-solving aspects of a quality system. By these and other means, the managers and staff, at all levels in a company, can develop a regard for quality; the need to strive for excellence in research, meeting or more than meeting clients' needs, working to the specification and maximising efficiency; all aspects of quality. However, for any of this to work, staff need the skills to perform their jobs in the best possible ways. Regardless of the morale level, quality cannot be delivered if the skills are not there and in the long run the frustration of a lack of skills will undermine morale.

To meet a short term need, some skills can be bought in. Staff can be hired to enable a company to offer a new sort of expertise and sometimes this is essential. If a quantitative agency decides to extend its services to qualitative research, there is no alternative but to recruit at least one or two key people. To fill a shorter-term need, temporary or freelance staff can be brought in. However, recruitment can never be the only or even the main means of building up skills. Existing staff have to be trained and their skills developed. This process has to be continuous because knowledge moves on relentlessly; no one ever knows enough or has enough applied skills. Even when new staff are taken on, they must also receive some in-house training to fit them into their new team. No company, least of all a market research agency, can, therefore, ever ignore training and staff development* entirely.

In one way or another all market research companies will train and develop their staff to a greater or lesser extent and spend money on this; even a short MRS course does not come cheap within the context of a smaller company. Training expenditure is, therefore, inevitable but it can easily be wasted. Spending more does not always mean better training; it all depends on how the training is managed. This can be illustrated by describing two models of training; a bad one and a better one.

Much of training carried out by market research agencies (and many other businesses) is unplanned and reactive. There is a recognition that skills and training are good things in general and there is some willingness to make money available and perhaps even set a budget. However, the training selected is unrelated to any broader planning of the company or even at the individual level. A common reason why someone goes on a particular training course is that a mail shot for it arrives or it is advertised in *MRS Research*, and a member of staff (or his or her manager) 'fancies the course'. In this way various members of staff are trained but no one considers priorities, whether the particular training initiatives actually deliver the skills promised or whether these are then used effectively. Eventually, during the year, the money runs out and training is put on hold. Perhaps any staff not receiving promised training are told that it will be their turn next year.

In case the reader is in any doubt, the above is the bad model of training. It may be an exaggeration. Perhaps even market research agencies are not that bad! But in many cases the organisation of training is probably not much better than this. So what is a better model?

---

* I shall not make a hard distinction between staff training and development. However, training can be thought of as shorter term, focused and delivered by a trainer in formal sessions, while development is more of a personal matter (though possibly with guidance), longer term and less focused.

The key difference is in planning, starting with what is needed. Once a year or perhaps even every quarter, the managers of the company need to consider what staff skills will be required. This may be over different timescales but perhaps most of the emphasis should be on the year ahead, if with some regard for the longer term. The skills considered will include, of course, professional market research expertise but also the skills required by other staff as well; interviewers, coders etc and in administration; secretaries, reception, accounts etc. As well as narrow functional skills, it may be important as well to think of more general ones such as IT or sales skills for staff involved with clients (this includes the receptionist too). The impact of new technology will also affect skill requirements; a switch to a computer on every desk may require professional staff to acquire basic keyboarding, CATI and CAPI will put new demands on interviewers etc. Above all, however, skill requirements cannot be divorced from other business planning. If the turnover objective for the coming year is a 20 per cent increase, where will the new business come from and what resources, including skills, will be needed to gain and deliver the extra business?

Once the needs are defined, the next step is a skill audit. To what extent are the required skills present already and what gaps exist? Such gaps can be both quantitative (numbers of staff with the skills) and qualitative (key skills entirely absent). Thought can then be given to how the gap is to be met. The two broad solutions are buying in – recruitment – or internal training. Qualitative gaps are more likely to involve the former, although there are no hard and fast rules. The training plan (but not the broader business plan), however, will be less concerned with the recruitment side.

So far the plan has been developed by the company's management without much staff involvement. Now is the time to consider the training needs of each individual member of staff. In a small company one manager can take on this task, but above a certain size the work will have to be delegated to departments. The best way of proceeding is by face to face meetings with individual staff. These can be informal or tied into such as an appraisal system; when past and future performance is being considered, training will inevitably have to be thought about.

Individual training needs can and should be considered in relation to three dimensions; the company's overall skill needs, the demands of the person's job and in terms of his or her own wishes and personal career development plans. The broad skill needs of the company should be known by this time and it is now a matter of seeing how the individual's skills can be developed accordingly. The demands of the job and the individual's performance may also define where further skilling is needed. Often skills are sufficient to perform the present job adequately but what

169

is needed to really excel or meet new needs as the job changes? Also a person planning a long term career with a company should be encouraged to think of the skills needed to move on into a new role. This then merges into personal wishes and ambitions; staff usually want training to improve their own employment position and earning potential. Usually company and personal plans can be reconciled, but this is not always the case and possibly some training or development cannot be sensibly accommodated, or at least substantially financed by the company. It may be very commendable that someone wishes to study Victorian art but the practical contribution to business growth may be limited.

With needs at both company and individual level defined, an action plan can be drawn up covering the forthcoming year and possibly longer ahead. The plan will set priorities in terms of what training is to be given, to whom and with a budget to pay for it (there may obviously have to be compromise and trade-off at this point). The methods of delivering training also need to be decided. This may involve sending staff on paid-for courses or bringing in a professional trainer. However, it is a mistake to assume that effective training has to always involve paid-for courses. In any company, there is always potential for skill and knowledge sharing; senior staff and staff who have been on external courses can hold their own seminars. There is also the development side; skills and knowledge can be self-taught and, in truth, any theoretical subject can often be as well mastered by old-fashioned reading as attending seminars. Informal coaching, hands-on learning and just 'sitting next to Nellie' are also effective means of skill delivery and the only drawback to them is that they are often not recognised for what they are. Staff may be well trained, but might not think of informal methods as training; it is hardly as exciting as going to a course run in a smart London hotel.

Training and development in market research should of course be linked into the profession and the programmes organised by the MRS. These include the many short courses organised every year but also the formal qualification system operated by MRS. There are two parallel routes; knowledge based leading up to the Diploma in Market Research and the competence based route of NVQs. The training of a company's staff can be linked to either of these routes and give individuals recognised and marketable qualifications as well as increasing their skill levels for day-to-day work. Of the two routes, the competence based NVQs are newer and to date have not really taken off. For whatever reason, companies have as yet shown little enthusiasm for putting staff into this programme. Professional training, however delivered, is important, but no company should limit its training plan to professional skills. Delivered quality is also very dependent on the skills of non-professional staff and even professional staff will need other skills (eg in IT, selling etc). Interviewers are a major group of non-professional staff and IQCS is very much concerned with skills of this sort and member companies will inevitably spend substantially on interviewer training and related appraisal; probably far more than the budget for professional staff.

To complete the training cycle, evaluation of the implemented plan is required, with any lessons learned applied to the next year's plan. First of all, it should be established whether the plan was substantially delivered. Perhaps for one reason or another some of the training was just never delivered. Why? There may have been good reasons and these should be considered next time round. Also the plan may have had to be changed to meet circumstances – the need for additional skills may have been recognised over the year. Planning is essential but it must not be so rigid that it cannot adapt as needs change.

Evaluation should also concern whether the training delivered was effective. This should involve the recipient's own judgements and this can be communicated informally or via such as course satisfaction scores etc. However, for the evaluation to be complete, there should also be a judgement on whether staff were not only happy with the courses etc but subsequently proved they applied new skills in the business. Sometimes, because of the time lag between training and application, this sort of judgement is difficult to make. It is also often difficult to measure improvements in performance resulting from training. In the case of simpler skills such as keyboarding it may be possible to measure productivity gains, but the benefits of more professional skills are much harder to quantify; there may be clear advances, but to what extent are these a direct result of training?

Finally there needs to be an evaluation of whether the overall training and development carried out over a year has made a positive contribution to the company's progress. Again much of this will have to be judgement rather than measurement, because causes and effects are often so difficult to separate. During the year the turnover targets may have been met, but how much of this is down to extra skilling and how much is the result of other factors such as better promotion, a strong economy or just self sustaining growth? However, difficult or not, overall evaluation is needed in order to sensibly plan next year's training and development.

In summary then this is the recommended 'better' model for training and development. It just so happens that the model put forward closely matches the Investors in People standard (all right, it is not entirely fortuitous that it does so) and in the next section I shall describe IiP and suggest that it can be usefully adopted by a market research company. The model (and IiP) also links into other standards. As discussed in Chapter 7, ISO 9000 has a requirement for training and this is mirrored in the MRQSA quality assurance model. The recommended training model and IiP dovetail into

ISO 9000/MRQSA but go beyond the rather limited requirements for training of these standards. A company carrying out training to the IiP standard will more than meet the requirements of ISO 9000/MRQSA. The standards for interviewer and supervisor training in IQCS and MRQSA can also be easily fitted into IiP.

INVESTORS IN PEOPLE

The IiP standard and scheme was launched by the Department of Employment in 1993 and has been administered through local TECs (Training and Enterprise Councils). Across all types of business the uptake has been considerable with some 4500 organisations recognised as Investors by late 1996 (ie they have been successfully assessed to the Standard) and a further 20,000 committed to the process. Several market research companies have implemented IiP and at the time of writing others are in the process of doing so.

The IiP standard (see Investors in People Unit, 1993) has four parts:

Investors in People – four parts of the standard

1. An Investor in People makes a public commitment from the top to develop all employees to achieve its business objectives.
2. An Investor in People regularly reviews the training and development needs of all employees.
3. An Investor in People takes action to train and develop individuals on recruitment and throughout their employment.
4. An Investor in People evaluates the investment in training and development to assess achievement and improve future effectiveness.

The Standard expands each part and defines indicators which are used in the assessment carried out for IiP recognition.

Commitment requires companies to have in place written business plans which alongside financial and other goals take into account training needs. Such plans can be in any format and may be spread over several documents which are part of more general ones (eg Board minutes); IiP requires some documentation, but it is not at all prescriptive about the form this takes. Commitment also implies some longer-term 'vision' of where the company is going and it is essential that this is effectively communicated to all staff (including the contribution they will make to realising it). Some sort of public mission or vision statement is probably needed although this should only symbolise it and not be taken to be the commitment. The vision, of course, does not have to be overambitious;

it is perfectly satisfactory if a company wishes to stay the same size. Commitment to growth is not essential and staying in business is an ambition of a sort. The indicators related to this part of the Standard cover visible evidence of the commitment (mission statements and the like and written plans) but also awareness among staff of the aims and vision of the organisation. When it comes to assessment, what staff know, believe and feel is as or more important as any documentation.

The requirements regularly to review training and development needs, require a company to have mechanisms in place to discuss these with each individual. However, this could be very informal with perhaps no more than a short note made after a meeting. The training needs should be related to both individual and corporate needs and managers need to also consider what resources will be needed to deliver the required training and development. It should not be assumed, however, that IiP necessarily involves spending any more on training; the same budget may just be spent more effectively. Responsibilities for implementation of training also need to be defined and understood – who will make sure it all happens? The assessment indicators required are broadly evidence of the above in various sorts of records as well as the manifest awareness and understanding by the staff involved. The Standard encourages the linking of training to NVQs (or SVQs in Scotland) although the qualification 'where appropriate' probably means that this is not essential if a good reason for not taking them up can be argued at assessment.

Taking action to train and develop staff has to cover both new recruits and existing workers. It is also indicated that staff should be encouraged to take some responsibility for their own training and development. Indicators in this case should show that things actually happen and include records of training, publicity given to development opportunities and evidence of management involvement.

The final part of the Standard concerns evaluation to assess what has been gained and to plan future training and development. Reviews should cover both the company and the individual level (and possibly departments in between). The senior management of the company is required to come to an overall judgement of the programme to date and draw implications for the future. Assessment indicators cover various types of evidence – documentary or otherwise – to show that this has been done.

As a document the IiP standard is relatively short (two pages only) and user friendly. There are no difficult terms and compared to, say, ISO 9000, the language is easy and non-technical. There is no need for any sort of 'translation' to relate the standard to the practices and structure of any particular industry. A fair criticism of the IiP standard, however, is that it can appear to repeat itself in several places, but this is quite easily untangled.

Implementing IiP is not particularly difficult for a company following something approaching the 'better model' of training as previously described. Providing there is commitment, planning, action and review and providing there is full staff involvement, little if anything will be needed specially to satisfy the IiP standard. Documents such as the business plan and records showing who was trained etc will be needed, but these can be in any form and do not need to measure up to any format requirements. Any company seriously committed to planned training will almost certainly maintain such records in some form. Compared to standards such as ISO 9000, IiP is non-prescriptive and very flexible. However, IiP is not in any sense an alternative to quality assurance systems. It addresses quality but from a different and complementary approach. There is no need for an ISO 9000 company to seek IiP or vice versa but the two hang together well. If a formal quality system to ISO 9000 (or MRQSA) is in place, it is sensible to integrate the documentation and records of training and development into the formal system. If the documents and records are needed they should be well kept and a formal quality system is, among other things, an effective way of ensuring this.

While IiP is flexible and non-bureaucratic, the need for commitment cannot be overemphasised. If a company believes ISO 9000 certification is a must, this can be obtained without either real commitment or effect on the business. It is possible to get by just going through the motions, even if this is very much a waste of effort. Playing at it, however, is not possible with IiP. Establishing true commitment and going behind paper records is very much at the heart of the assessment process.

A timetable for implementation of an IiP programme is needed and realistically this takes a complete planning cycle – a calendar or financial year for most companies. At the start of the year training is planned as part of the overall business plan. Meetings with staff as well as management time will also be necessary. Over the year the plan is put into action and towards the end of the period a review is completed ready for the cycle to start again. Only at this point is the company ready for assessment.

IiP is very much a local TEC product and help in implementation is available in various forms including general advice, seminars and workshops and possibly assistance towards the costs of one-to-one consultancy. Many consultancies offer their services to companies seeking IiP, although this sort of assistance is by no means essential and less so than in the case of ISO 9000. Regardless of the need for assistance, any company wishing to seek IiP needs to contact the local TEC early on and effectively register a commitment to the programme.

ASSESSMENT TO IiP

Assessment is carried out by independent consultants appointed by local TECs with the ultimate decision to award IiP recognition in the hands of a panel of local notables meeting under the TEC's auspices.

The form of the assessment, but not the content, is similar to ISO 9000 assessment. In this case the off-site 'desk investigation' involves examining a portfolio of evidence put together by the company seeking assessment. In theory at least, the portfolio should contain little material prepared specially for the assessment and is instead mainly copies of documents produced in planning, delivering and evaluating training. Examples of material that might be contained include; a brief background on the company and its business (a sales brochure could well meet this need), an internal structure chart, organisation and staff names (eg from the phone list), the business and training plan, the vision or mission statement, copies of other quality related documents (eg an ISO 9000 certificate), a summary of any review carried out by senior management of the effectiveness of the training completed (this might be an extract of Board minutes), and samples taken from records of staff appraisals or training planning meetings and the details of training received. In summary, whatever gives a picture of how training and development works in the company. Unless it is very deficient, the portfolio of evidence is not regarded as evidence of compliance or otherwise with the Standard (as is ISO 9000 documentation). Rather it is used by the assessor to structure the on-site assessment.

The on-site assessment may take several days for a medium-sized research company and rather longer for the largest or those with several sites. Small companies though may be completed in a day or two. Most of the time during the assessment is taken up with discussions and meetings and involves as many staff as possible. Compared with ISO 9000, there is a larger subjective element with the assessor seeking to establish that the company is 'for real' – that the plans are not just documents but lead to action, that managers ensure things happen and staff are aware and understand their involvement in both training and realising the company's vision. Evidence of positive attitudes by the workforce to training and the business as a whole contributes to a successful assessment but a complete lack of dissonance between workers and management is not demanded. Realistically it is recognised that not everyone can be happy with their own or general employment conditions all of the time. During the year it may have been necessary (or thought to be necessary) for the management to take decisions which were not welcomed by sections of the staff. Nor is there any need to hide the 'awkward squad' from the assessor.

On completion, the assessor is likely to indicate his or her view of the company in relation to IiP but the formal decision is taken by the local TEC panel. If all goes well the company receives the IiP plaque and has the right to display the logo. Unlike ISO 9000, there are no follow up surveillance visits twice a year. After three years, however, the assessment must be repeated, in full, to retain IiP recognition.

Assessment has a cost. Assessors charge consultant level rates. However, it may be possible to obtain assistance from the local TEC towards the costs involved.

IS IiP WORTH HAVING?

Being a recognised Investor has some kudos and may impress clients or even potential staff to some extent. However, it is very doubtful that work will be gained just on the strength of the plaque (as it may be with ISO 9000). If IiP is worth having, it must be because the processes involved, and which are necessary to meet the standard, produce benefits quite unrelated to assessment or recognition. If a company is following anything approaching the suggested 'better model' of training it will be doing nearly everything needed to gain IiP recognition. And the commitment to training, implicit in the model, is in any case essential to deliver quality and pursue business success. Therefore, why not seek IiP recognition? There will be some assessment costs but the kudos that is gained – and this includes internally as well as externally – will be at least commensurate. Extra management time involved in understanding and seeking assessment should be minimal. Management time will certainly be taken up in planning and delivering training but if this cannot be spared there is little long-term hope to improve quality or for that matter to develop the business at all.

The above are essentially negative arguments to seek recognition. In addition, the process of seeking IiP is itself a spur to action. Training and development are of course essential but the prospect of assessment gives that extra reason for doing things right and doing them when they should be done. Like ISO 9000, IiP helps us to be virtuous.

11

Quality and international research

There is probably no developed or even developing country without some sort of market research industry. Worldwide, the value of market research has been estimated at around £9000 million of which the USA market is worth £3500 million, Europe £3800 million, the Far East £800 million, with £1000 million for the rest of the world. The future demand for market research, worldwide, is likely to continue to grow and particularly in rapidly emerging economies such as China. Much of the £3500 million spent on market research is still accounted for by local and national studies but, with globalisation, the demand for international research – usually covering a number of countries, but rarely truly worldwide – accounts for an ever increasing share of market research spend. In 1995 for example, international research valued at just over £100 million accounted for 27 per cent of the total turnover of UK, AMSO research companies* and this sort of work was 20 per cent higher in value than in the previous year. Research is also provided through international research companies and networks; several of the largest UK companies can offer research in most major countries using the resources of other members of their own groups.

International research of course involves all the quality issues of domestic projects but with some additional concerns as well and it is these, and possible solutions, which are discussed in this chapter.

---

* The UK market research industry has a strong share of international research; above its natural 'weight'.

QUALITY ISSUES IN INTERNATIONAL RESEARCH

A user of international research seeks data and findings from each country covered in a project, which are equally valid and are comparable. In practice there are several barriers to achieving this. These include some lack of agreement between countries on what constitutes valid research practice, cultural differences standing in the way of comparable data and differences in how research is organised and structured around the world and even within regions such as Europe.

Since there is some lack of agreement about what constitutes valid research design within the UK, it is hardly surprising to find even greater differences internationally. And as Taylor describes, these are not trivial differences:

> ... survey methods which are standard practice in some countries are regarded as gross malpractice in others (Taylor, 1995).

Areas of divergence singled out by Taylor – principally in opinion poll research where inaccuracy of results is both measurable and public – include the use (or rejection) of quota sampling, random dialling in phone research and weighting techniques. In these and other areas, a survey of leading research companies around the world showed that practices and belief in what is valid vary widely, with, for example, US researchers working in a very different way to Europeans.

To some extent, the differences may be defended as reflecting local conditions. Random sampling used widely in the US is rather less practical in countries lacking adequate sampling frames such as up-to-date electoral registers. Phone research depends on high levels of phone penetration and so on. However, the differences cannot be wholly or even mainly explained by practicalities. At least equally important is the tradition and professional standing of research within each country and these may affect not only what is considered 'true' but also the importance attached to an ideal of true and right research. However, truth and rightness are at the heart of quality as excellence and it is hard to believe that the intellectual foundations of research depend on national characteristics.

Leaving aside the fundamentals of research design, there are also practical difficulties in comparing data and findings between countries and the most obvious is the language barrier. Excepting such as retail auditing, market research is language bound. It is carried out through and understood in terms of language, yet in most international research projects data have to be collected in different languages. This leads to practical issues of translation. It is hard enough to get the questionnaire wording right in one language, let alone half a dozen, and quite small variations may well affect the comparability of the data. Quality control of some sort is clearly needed in translations at the questionnaire design stage to cover not only who does the initial work but also how this is checked and validated. The practical difficulties of organising this are serious enough where major languages are involved but obviously even more so with the more obscure* ones. Simply leaving interviewers to translate from the original questionnaire is certainly not enough even if the individuals concerned are reasonably fluent in both languages (this is not an uncommon practice in international phone research conducted from one site). Language is also an issue at the back-end of a research project; in data processing. There are various ways of handling translation at the coding stage for example and these have also given rise to quality and comparability questions (see Owen, 1991).

There are also other cultural differences which are important in carrying out and comparing international research. Who can be interviewed by whom and where, for example, may be an issue in Islamic or other countries. Even the cultural meaning of questions and responses is by no means universal; responses to please the interviewer, for example, are more likely in some places than others. Nor should it be assumed that the concept of randomness and 'equality' of respondents is necessarily accepted. In some countries the idea of seeking the opinions of a random sample rather than of 'informed' or 'advanced' respondents is not readily understood. Given issues of this sort, a standardised methodology and questionnaire may sometimes produce data less valid and comparable than where the research design is varied to reflect cultural differences.

Research is also structured and organised in different ways in different countries and the most quality sensitive aspect of this is the role and status of interviewers. The nature of interviewers' employment, their pay and how they are trained, supervised and their work validated are all critical to the research outcome. As discussed in earlier chapters, structural factors of the UK industry give rise to quality concerns about primary research data. UK practice in interviewer quality control, including through the IQCS initiative, however, is probably at the top end of any international scale in this respect and the practices in some countries are likely to be poor enough to lead to serious doubts about the reliability of the input data.

---

* Obscure is meant in a purely practical sense and no cultural judgement is intended. English is obscure if English translators are not available.

IMPROVING QUALITY IN INTERNATIONAL RESEARCH

Many of the quality problems in international research reflect the lack of common approaches and, where it is appropriate, standardisation. Obviously any standardisation of practice needs to be at a best practice rather than lowest common denominator level.

The commercial organisation of international research will to some extent lead to standardisation without any broader approaches. The large global research companies will inevitably tend to standardise their approaches and methods in each country where they operate. Companies such as the Cantar Group (owned by WPP) with a base in the UK, IPSOS and Sofres in France, Infratest Burke in Germany and Nielsen in the US are likely to favour similar methods of working wherever surveys are conducted, although with local adaptations as needed. Apart from quality issues, commercial advantage will favour standardisation in some areas (eg data processing) and with knock-on effects to other operations. Through a trickle down affect, the standardisation of the large companies will also effect how smaller companies work and will, in the long run, tend to promote convergence in practice.

Other mechanisms of international standardisation will include initiatives specific to particular areas of research. The work of International Broadcasting Audience Research is one example of this (see Myton, 1996). There are also the international research forums which will at least highlight the problem areas if not always solve them. These include ESOMAR (based on individual membership) and EFEMRA (a federation of national European market research trade associations). There is also now a European and wider interest in developing international service standards for market research, mirroring and initiated by MRQSA.

All this begs the question of what will be standardised. One possibility is standardisation of research design principles with the techniques based on global criteria of validity. This will happen to some extent within international research groups where it would be difficult to offer global clients solutions based on different concepts of what is right research in different countries. Beyond this change, however, it is harder to see convergence in the medium term. Even within one country, such as the UK, there is considerable debate on what constitutes valid research. Also the intellectual traditions on which market research is based are often different across cultures. It may even be that the search for this sort of fundamental standardisation is a chimera and if attained would be undesirable. Different traditions, stronger or weaker in different countries, may each offer a different sort of illumination. The ongoing contacts between national bodies, the exchange of information and articles for the learned journals and the international conferences organised by bodies such as ESOMAR, at least allow for an understanding of the differences and may encourage convergence in some areas.

A more practical prospect is standardisation in areas such as how clients' requirements are identified and met, the effective execution of a research design and services provided to clients apart from those based on right research methods. In other words the areas which are being addressed in the UK through MRQSA's service standards. Some standardisation in these areas does look to be a practical goal since, in the relatively short time since its publication, there has been considerable interest across Europe and elsewhere in MRQSA standards. Several national trade bodies have indicated a wish to adopt the standards with or without modification. A major element in the MRQSA (taken from IQCS) is of course minimum standards for data collection. More than anything else, an expectation that fieldwork will be carried out to recognised and known minimum standards could lead to significant actual and perceived improvements in the quality of international research. However, in some countries the changes in fieldwork practices which will be required to approach MRQSA/IQCS standards will not be quickly or easily brought about. Commercial considerations as well as any commitment to quality will effect the rate of change. Clearly a move to standardise in this and similar areas will favour countries and companies which already implement the standards over those who will need to spend substantially to bring their practice into line. And nor is the attempt to standardise fieldwork quality new. In 1989 Janet Weitz argued the case for Europe-wide adoption of IQCS standards (see Weitz, 1989).

A possible longer-term outcome might be an 'official' service standard for market research under the authority of the bodies responsible for harmonisation and development of quality standards at European (CEN) or international levels (ISO). Some interest in reaching this has already been expressed in forums such as EFEMRA and ESOMAR. With this potential interest, MRQSA in the UK has started to redraft its standards, with BSI support, as a British Standard so that it is in a format which could be adopted by CEN or ISO. In the meantime, MRQSA needs to take more account of the special requirements of international research and incorporate relevant requirements in areas such as translation; to date these issues have been neglected.

12

Developing a quality system

In this final chapter, I provide some practical guidance on developing a quality system. Such systems are not the only route to quality. Other approaches have an important role in market research. However, for a business above even a quite small size, some systematic approach to maintaining quality is required and, even if it is not recognised as such, a system will evolve. An effective quality system is also a requirement of MRQSA standards and it appears likely that these will be increasingly recognised within the UK and possibly the international research industry.

STANDARDS AND THE SYSTEM

Two different sorts of standards are relevant to a quality system and the relevance of each needs to be understood at the outset. There are the standards for the system itself and there are the service or product standards which are incorporated into the system.

The two relevant standards for a quality system in a market research company are ISO 9001 or 9002 and the quality assurance element of MRQSA, which as explained in Chapter 9 is rather more limited in scope than ISO 9000. In either case, however, these standards prescribe the form and scope of a system to manage quality and to ensure constant and consistent quality levels, without specifying what the latter should be. At some early point, a decision needs to be made on which of these two models for a quality system will be followed. However, the choice is not once and for all; the MRQSA quality assurance model can, at a later time, be uprated to meet ISO 9001 or 9002 and if the ISO 9000 models are used the system will meet the requirements of MRQSA whether or not ISO 9000 assessment is sought.

The relevant service or product standards which the system is to incorporate and implement may obviously include MRQSA. These standards for the whole research process include data collection and in effect IQCS. A quality system could also incorporate IQCS standards but not the other major areas covered by MRQSA. However, given developments, it might seem perverse to develop a quality system meeting IQCS but not the standards for executive services or data processing (assuming the latter is an in-house activity). The system can also embody all the professional code requirements of MRS or ESOMAR, although the parts of the codes which apply to the activities of companies rather than just individuals are, in any case, linked into MRQSA. The requirements of Investors in People can also be built into procedures even though this standard does not itself require a formal, procedure based, system to be in place.

Apart from external standards such as MRQSA, a company may well wish to incorporate its own 'standards' into a quality system and these may well be higher in some way or other than MRQSA requirements. Each and every company will have its own ways of working which are believed to add to the quality of service offered to its clients and in most cases it will be appropriate to incorporate these precepts into a formal quality system. However, a word of warning at this point. The core of a quality system is a set of mandatory procedures which are to be followed in all relevant cases. A system is not just 'good practice'. Requirements should, therefore, not be put into a system unless they are considered to be essential and unless compliance can realistically be expected. It is one thing to set rules and quite another matter to follow them.

QUALITY SYSTEM PROCEDURES

For most practical purposes, the physical embodiment of the quality system is a set or sets of procedures and most of the effort required to develop an effective system will go into planning, drafting and successfully implementing these documents. An understanding of procedures is, therefore, needed at the start of any project to develop an effective quality system.

Procedures* are working methods or rules to be followed in carrying out a process such as preparing proposals, coding, data entry etc. They

---

* Specimen procedures are provided in the appendix. These are provided so that the reader can see examples of complete procedure sets, rather than as a model to neccesarily copy; other layouts and formats are every bit as good as the specimens.

describe key steps in the process which are considered essential for quality or other (eg financial control or safety) reasons. However, procedures are not necessarily comprehensive; they do not specify everything that has to be done since it is assumed that they are followed by trained and skilled staff. A proposal procedure will, therefore, specify some important steps such as the scope of the document, who prepares it, who checks it etc, but it will not be of any practical value unless the person drafting the document has the necessary research and writing skills. A procedure set, therefore, is not a training manual, although it may well be useful as an aid in training (eg introducing skilled but new staff to how a particular process is followed in the company).

The quality standards to be implemented through the quality system are embedded into the procedures but in a way which is unique to the particular business. The MRQSA standards for example specify (in paragraph 3.1) that 'the supplier shall have in place defined methods of checking resources and available expertise before responding to a client's requirement and brief'. A company's procedures meeting this standard will describe and specify these methods and, whatever these are, they will be prescribed and intended to be always followed whenever a proposal or quotation is prepared. Procedures are, therefore, mandatory and uniform; whenever the circumstances to which they relate arise (eg a client request) all staff involved are expected to follow the steps and do the things which are required. The corollary, of this, however, is that procedures should be minimal; they should not specify more than is considered essential. Procedures, therefore, should not include 'guidelines' or 'good practice' since in neither case are these, by definition, essential or mandatory statements. Similarly, phrases such as 'wherever possible' and similar should be avoided since non-compliance can always be justified on grounds of 'not possible'.

An extension of mandatory procedures is auditability. It should be possible to establish, after the event, whether or not the procedure has been followed; some record should be left. If this is not the case and there is no way of knowing whether or not it has been followed, the procedure is useless. However, this does not and should not imply that every procedure (or even the very large majority) requires a separate 'form' to be completed – in most research processes the 'mark' of the procedure can either be left on documents produced as part of the process itself, questionnaires, proposals etc, or by 'signing-off' a checklist covering many procedures.

The last general point to make about procedures concerns the usage of the singular and plural cases. The distinction is only nominal but practically useful. A single 'procedure' can usefully be thought of as relating to a specific operation – eg numbering and batching completed questionnaires – and the step can be described in one or two sentences, eg: 'The questionnaires relating to a project will be uniquely and sequentially numbered as received, by the Data Entry Clerk, secured into batches and with each batch fronted with a Batch Sheet'. A number of such procedures relating to a series of linked operations can be regarded as a 'procedure set'; the procedure about numbering and batching might for example form part of a procedure set covering 'data entry set up'. Finally, procedure sets can be linked into sections and then into a complete procedure manual covering the whole business. The numbering system used for procedures can follow this hierarchy, eg:

- 6.   Data Entry procedures [section].
- 6.1   Data Entry Set Up procedures [procedure set].
- 6.1.1 Numbering and Batching procedure [procedure].

These then are some essential or recommended features of procedures, but what about the contents? What should be actually set out in a procedure or procedure set? Obviously the specific contents depend on what is covered, but regardless of where they are applied, well designed and effective procedures should always communicate five things:

Procedure coverage

1. Where/when the procedure applies.
2. Who is responsible for carrying out the procedure.
3. Who checks that the procedure has been followed (if this is considered to be essential).
4. What has to be done.
5. What evidence there is of compliance (and what form this takes).

Where and when the procedure applies is defined in terms of the processes carried out and possibly in terms of the department responsible, although it is not usually desirable to tie procedures to a specific organisational structure. The procedure for numbering and batching questionnaires, for example, applies whenever completed questionnaires are received. Some procedures may be relevant to every project carried out while others may only apply in a certain sort of work. In either case this should be clear in the procedure, eg in a description of the 'scope' of the procedure.

Who is responsible for implementing the procedure (job title rather than name) should also always be specified; whose job is it to ensure that whatever needed doing is done? This may be defined under a separate heading or within the text of other parts of the procedures. Similarly responsibility for checking that the procedure is followed should also be set out, but only where such a check is considered essential; in most cases it will not be.

Naturally, the procedure should describe what actually has to be done – eg 'each questionnaire will be uniquely and sequentially numbered' – but only in the detail needed by a trained operator (ie it is assumed that the operator knows specifically how the numbering is applied). This description may well also specify or imply the evidence of compliance with the procedure – in the example the evidence is the numbering applied to the questionnaire and completion of the Batch Sheet. Where forms or special record sheets are required by the procedure (eg the Batch Sheet), it is good practice to number these in a way that relates to the procedure concerned, eg if the procedure is numbered 6.1.1, the Batch Sheet can be numbered 6.1.1/1.

Many different formats can be used for procedures and none is intrinsically superior provided it adequately communicates the range of contents discussed above. The specimen procedures in the Appendix are just one model and they do not have to be followed in detail. Inevitably some words will be used in procedures but these can be supplemented with figures, flow diagrams or other aids. Since procedures are meant to communicate effectively, words should be simple and in short sentences and paragraphs, with any technical terms, which may be in doubt, defined. However, what is 'technical' is determined by context and experience; a term may be fully understood internally but obscure to outsiders (in which case definition is less important than in the converse case).

Quality system documentation, including procedures, needs to be controlled. Since procedures are meant to be mandatory and uniform, it is very important that everyone in a company follows the same version. When a quality system is first introduced, this is not a major problem because there is only one version (although even in this case there may be various preliminary drafts before the final and agreed version). As time goes on, however, the procedures will need changing; changing to improve them, to take account of changing circumstances or of changes in the standards being applied. It will then be important that, from an agreed date, it is the revised, rather than the superseded, version which is used. There are various formatting devices to aid document control (see also the specimen procedures) including version numbering, together with a master list of the latest versions, dating at the time of issue, giving one person the authority to issue procedures and page numbering so that it is clear whether or not pages are missing (eg page 1/3 means the first page of a set of three). However, a more radical solution to document control is to have the procedures on-screen only and avoid paper copies entirely; if a computer network is already installed this may be the better approach, provided everyone requiring to use procedures has practical access to the network.

DEVELOPING PROCEDURES

Developing a complete set or manual of procedures, from scratch, to provide the documentary basis for a quality system will be a major project in any business. The first step is commitment; the company as a whole must believe this to be an important task and as far as possible everyone needs to understand why a formal system is being introduced. However, as well as general support, one person needs to be given the responsibility for seeing the project through to completion and preferably within an agreed timetable. This person needs to be senior enough to drive the work forward even when other things – particularly day-to-day business – are pressing and to have access to all necessary resources. The project leader, however, does not have to do all the work personally. Much of the labour involved is taken up by procedure drafting and, as will be argued shortly, it is far better to delegate this work. Outside consultants can also be brought in to assist in the work although it is important that the ownership of the system is internal. Having consultants sit in a corner and draft some procedures is not a recipe for a successful system. If used, consultants should be facilitators and not primarily doers.

Procedures need to be planned within three sets of parameters:

Procedure planning parameters

1. Existing practice of the business.
2. The requirements of external standards to be applied to the quality system.
3. Other (internal) requirements.

In the initial stages of planning procedures, the most important of these parameters is the existing practice of the business; how the major processes of the business are currently carried out. Only after these are analysed, understood and set out in simple chart form should the requirements of external standards or additional internal requirements be considered. It is better to start with what exists (and probably works well) than try and remake the whole organisation from first principles. Moreover, it is very likely that most of the practices required by the external standards such as MRQSA are already followed in practice and the only major change required is to document what is already done.

Simple charting, which requires no great skill, is by far the best tool for the type of analysis required and the focus should be the processes carried out rather than the departmental arrangements of the business, since the former are more fundamental and lasting than the latter. The processes can be viewed at different levels of generality, with charting built up on a Russian doll approach. Figure 12.1 represents the processes

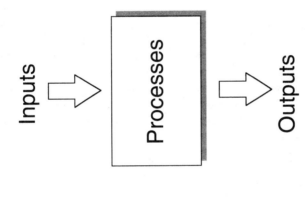

Figure 12.1 *Business analysis chart – level 1*

of any business at the most general level; inputs come into the business, they are processed and outputs go out. In a market research company, the inputs may include client briefs, bought-in expertise, materials of various sorts and from time to time pieces of equipment such as computers. The internal processes cover everything that is done to produce a client service and the outputs are the documents and other communication delivered to clients. However, representation at so general a level is of little use except as an aid to thinking of the business from a process rather than an organisational perspective.

Figure 12.2 is rather more specific and unique and illustrates the business as a series of major processes; marketing (to generate enquiries), proposal drafting and fundamental research design etc.

However, each process in Figure 12.2 can be analysed in further detail and as a set of subprocesses; Figure 12.3 shows in more detail what happens in data processing. And nor need we stop there; Figure 12.4 shows the coding operation within data processing and even this can be quite sensibly analysed further (as in Figure 12.5) to show suboperations such as developing the coding frame (which too can be analysed further should this be useful).

The greater the analysis detail, the more work involved and the more specific knowledge needed. Any senior member of staff is likely to be able to produce the sort of analysis represented by Figure 12.2 quite easily and quickly. They may, however, need assistance from a department manager to chart Figure 12.3 and corresponding representations of other major processes. At the level of Figures 12.4 and 12.5, even the data processing manager will probably need to consult other staff – those involved in the actual operations – and this is no bad thing; it both improves understanding and creates involvement from those who will eventually be expected to follow the new procedures. At this stage it is important as far as possible to show what actually happens rather than what it is thought ought to happen. Difficulties arise, however, where the practice varies widely and randomly.

The charting stage of procedure planning may take some time to complete but it is arguably the most important part of the work. Only once current practice is understood can any changes needed to meet external standards or other requirements be sensibly considered. However, it is not essential to analyse the whole operation in complete detail at one time. Having gone to the detail represented by say levels two and three (Figures 12.2 and 12.3), further analysis can be carried out sequentially with procedures drafted for one major process before starting on another.

With a thorough analysis of existing practice complete, attention can turn to the changes needed to comply with the standards to be adopted.

190

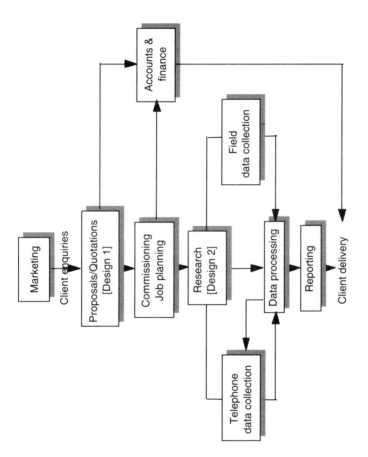

Figure 12.2 *Business analysis chart – level 2*

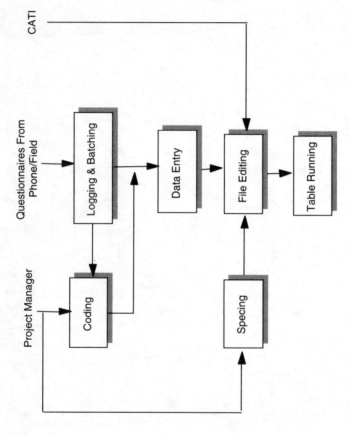

Figure 12.3 *Business analysis chart – level 3 (data processing)*

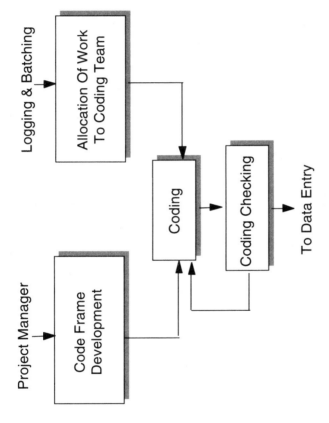

Figure 12.4 *Business analysis chart – level 4 (coding)*

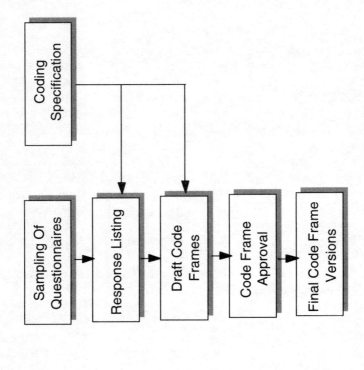

Figure 12.5 *Business analysis chart – level 5 (coding frame)*

Using a copy of MRQSA or other standards to be adopted, each requirement can be matched against current practice and the gaps highlighted. Current practice can also be compared with purely internal requirements for quality improvements which in specific areas may go beyond what is prescribed in the external standards. The process of analysis and generally thinking about quality problems will also stimulate many proposals and suggestions. However, some caution is recommended at this stage. Developing a quality system for the first time, to meet external standards, is enough of a task to be taking on without creating all manner of additional hurdles. Also, it should be recognised that while enthusiasm for quality improvement is to be welcomed, once incorporated into procedures the suggestions will become mandatory and possibly seem less of a good idea. In general, the best advice is to create the new system around what absolutely has to be done and once it is working then make changes to bring about desired quality improvements.

While process charting is strongly recommended, it may be found that some of the requirements of external standards such as MRQSA and ISO 9000, for which procedures will be needed, do not appear on the business 'map'. This is because these relate to support activities carried out within the company but which may not be regarded as a direct part of the core businesses processes. The two main activities of this sort are purchasing and training. Again, however, some practice in these areas will be established and can be simply described in chart or word form and compared with the requirements to identify gaps where changes will be needed to meet the external standards. Finally there are some formal requirements of external standards that will need to be met and for which procedures are required but for which, almost certainly, nothing at all will be in place before the system is developed. They arise because a quality system is developed and there are various mechanisms to ensure the system is effective. Examples are management of the system, methods of controlling documents and making changes to the system (both of these link together), internal auditing and procedures to investigate and solve quality problems.

With the map and descriptions of the business and comparisons made with the requirements of external standards, the procedures can now be planned. A list of the procedures required can be drawn up and a provisional numbering system devised. The work of actually drafting the procedures can then be allocated and the project leader is strongly urged not to take on all this work since wide involvement throughout the company is far better. Data entry procedures for example are best written by the manager responsible, since he or she will have a better understanding of the details of the process. Even more importantly, however, the data entry procedures will be 'owned' rather than imposed and if they prove unworkable who can the data entry manager blame but him or herself? The same principle applies throughout the company.

Obviously, before the procedure drafting team starts work, some briefing will be required, including a discussion of where existing practice needs extending or changing to meet requirements. One or more model procedures should also be drafted by the project leader as a pattern for others to follow and to ensure a common format to the procedures. There is in fact no absolute requirement for a common format to procedures but it is strongly recommended; they are easier to control and, because they are more obviously procedures, are more likely to be followed. Once drafted, the procedures should also be tested – as far as possible, have relevant staff attempt to follow and work to them; often this will highlight problems which may never have occurred to the drafters. Finally, someone should formally approve each procedure set in readiness for its issue and implementation.

OTHER DOCUMENTATION

While procedures are the core of a documented quality system, other material will be required as well, either for practical reasons or because of requirements of external standards. ISO 9001 or 9002, for example, require a quality manual (as well as procedures) containing a formal description of how the standard is implemented and this should include a written quality policy (see Chapters 7 and 8).

More practical and everyday documentation includes forms and record sheets used to record the progress of a job and the results of checks and validation work carried out. These will normally be designed as part of the procedures and, as discussed previously, should be kept to a minimum. Some form of checklist, signed-off as each stage is complete and as each check or test is made, can cover most of the project related record requirements as well as provide a quick indication of the stage reached in a project. An example of such a checklist is included in the Appendix.

A filing system for records also needs to be considered. Almost inevitably this will include job files of one sort or another containing all quality records relating to a specific project. It is of course quite possible to have this file largely or entirely in electronic form and commonly accessible though a local computer network. If such networking is well established, the system can be wholly electronic from the start and as well as records can include the procedures themselves. However, this should only be attempted where a network is well established, practicably accessible to all staff and backed with in-house IT expertise.

Records and filing will revolve around a job numbering system. This cannot be avoided and in a company of any size is unlikely to be a new concept. There will be, however, additional reasons to ensure job numbers are used accurately and recorded on all project related material.

QUALITY SYSTEM IMPLEMENTATION

I probably overlaboured some of the points about developing a quality system. Documents and their design are a stock in trade of market research and I would be surprised if any research company, even with only limited coaching and support, will find such a project beyond their capabilities (it may be beyond their practical capacity because of the time required etc but this is a different issue). For market research companies, unlike some other types of businesses, procedure drafting and system development should be a relatively easy task. However, a quality system is not just a work of literature. To be effective it has to be implemented and followed and in my experience this is the harder part; people such as research executives are first rate when it comes to planning systems and finding creative solutions to quality problems, but less reliable at actually doing what is required, each and every time.

Clearly staff cannot be expected to work to procedures unless they know what these are. The written procedures need, therefore, to be available around the company. These should be 'official' and controlled copies and the use of other versions or copies should be discouraged (this is an issue of document control). However, this is not enough. Even though researchers are nearly all well educated and can be assumed to be literate, it seems to be unrealistic to assume that staff will actually read procedures. Training sessions are, therefore, essential and these need to be repeated at regular intervals to both bring new staff into the system and reinvigorate long-standing staff.

With the procedures finalised, printed and circulated and with staff trained in working to the procedures, the new system can be formally launched. The choice is between the 'big bang' approach of a 'Q' day or to have implementation on a roll-out basis a department at a time. Both approaches have advantages as well as drawbacks. In either case, however, the system needs monitoring to ensure it is working, and this is the role of internal auditing.

AUDITING

Internal auditing is a requirement of ISO 9001 or 9002 but not of MRQSA standards. However, a quality system has to be monitored in some way if it is to work at all. This can be done fairly informally, but it is usually better to adopt a more formal internal auditing procedure (one of the specimen procedures in the Appendix covers the audit process); the work involved is no more than if it is carried out informally and formality will ensure that it is done regularly. There is not space here to describe internal auditing in any detail (see Jackson and Ashton, 1995) but in principle it involves comparing practice against what is required by the written procedures. The auditing process is carried out by trained staff* who are independent of the area audited (eg data processing staff do not audit data processing) and the objective is to compare practice with requirements and note any differences. The auditors' role stops at this point; it is not their job to understand why the system is not working as required and still less to propose solutions or apportion blame. Significant problems ('non-conformities') should then be investigated by someone other than the auditor and following procedures for quality improvement or corrective action. Once action has been taken, it is good practice to re-audit the area to establish whether the action has proved to be effective.

Auditing needs to be planned so that all the company and all the system are covered at least once in a year and a new system should be audited completely as soon as possible after implementation and before external assessment.

ASSESSMENT

Although, as argued in other chapters, the major benefit from a quality system should be improvements rather than a certificate, companies meeting ISO 9001 or 9002 or MRQSA standards are very likely to seek assessment. Some period of 'running-in' is required between implementation of the system and its assessment, but six months will be long enough to wait in most cases. When the system is complete, or even before, an assessment body needs selecting and terms agreeing; there is often a problem arranging an assessment date at short notice. The list at the end of Chapter 9 provides contact details for MRQSA approved assessment bodies (as at the end of 1996) and each of these can also assess market research companies to ISO 9001 or 9002. A company seeking assessment to both sets of standards will obviously wish to combine the process.

DEVELOPING SYSTEMS

---

* Adequate training can be carried out internally although there are many short courses offered in this area.

Quality systems should never be regarded as final and fixed. Rather they should constantly evolve to overcome internal problems (eg a procedure proves not to work well), to meet changes in external standards, to adjust to changes in the processes and organisation of the business and last, but most important of all, to make quality improvements. Opportunities for improvements may be identified through internal auditing, client comments (or complaints) or just through suggestions. Whatever the source, however, the system should include mechanisms for reviewing proposed changes and improvements and then formal incorporation so that the 'better way' is followed constantly and consistently.

Finally an established system may need developing to bring it into line with another set of external standards. Systems to ISO 9001 or 9002, for example, will require modification so that they also meet MRQSA standards. However, the changes in this case are unlikely to be very extensive and a company already familiar with a quality system to ISO 9001 or 9002 will have no problem managing the changes required in the system. However, to state what should be obvious, the same documented system should cover both sets of standards; the internal procedures should be seamless rather than having separate bits for ISO 9000 and MRQSA.

Appendix:
Specimen procedures

PROCEDURE 1.1

COMMISSIONING

Purpose

To ensure all projects are effectively managed, are identified by a unique Job Number an(
that a Job File is kept recording the completion of all relevant steps in the Quality System

Scope

All projects carried out.

References

The Quality Manual
Procedure Manuals: 1.0, 6.5

Definitions

Documentation

Project Manager's Checklist 1.1.6/1

QS 1.1	.	Revision: Date: Written by: P Jackson Reason of issue: Original Authority:	Page 1/3

1.1.1   Project Manager

A Quality Director shall, on commission, appoint or confirm a suitable person to act as Project Manager for the project and record this by signing the Project Manager's Checklist (see 1.1.6) in the appropriate place.

The project manager may be a member of staff or a freelance, outside supplier in which case the purchasing procedure (6.5) must be followed including in the selection of suppliers from the Approved Supplier List (see 6.5.2/1) or from the Probationary Supplier List (see 6.5.4/1) and the completion of a written Supplier Order (see 6.5.6/1) which shall be given to the supplier with a copy filed in the Job File (see 1.1.4).

A Quality Director may at any time exercise the responsibilities of the Project Manager in relation to any project (eg sign as and for the Project Manager).

1.1.2   Job Identification

The Project Manager must ensure that every commissioned job is given a unique job number and that this is used on all relevant documentation and records relating to the job. Normally the job number on commission will be the same as given to the proposal/quotation (see 1.0.2).

1.1.3   Job Card And Job Log Update

The Project Manager will ensure that the Job Card (1.0.6/1) and the Job Log (1.0.1/2) - commission date and Project Manager - are updated. The updated Job Card shall be placed, as soon as possible, in a commissioned job rack and kept there at all times when not being further updated.

1.1.4   Job File

The Project Manager shall prepare, as soon as possible, label (to show the Job Number and Project Manager) and open a Job File.

In the case of consultancy and similar jobs where the normal processes (including data collection/data processing) are not involved a job file need not be prepared or used.

QS 1.1   Revision:
Date:
Written by: P Jackson
Reason of issue: Original
Authority:
Page 2/3

203

1.1.5   Job File Responsibility

The Project Manager shall be responsible for keeping the Job File updated (as quickly as possible) and ensuring as far as practical, it is available to all staff requiring to consult it.

1.1.6   Project Manager's Checklist

A Project Manager's Checklist (1.1.6/1) shall be attached to each Job File with the top labelling completed. The Project Manger shall be responsible for making entries on the Project Manager's Checklist to show that procedures have been followed and the progress of the job. Where a procedure is not relevant to a job a "N/A" entry shall be made on the checklist.

1.1.7   Client Written Orders

Where the client sends a written order for the commission this document shall be attached to the Job File.

1.1.8   Deposit Invoicing

The project Manger shall ensure that the deposit invoice (or any intermediate invoices) which is part of the terms of the contract with the client is sent to the client as soon as possible after commission. Appropriate entries shall be made on the Job Card (1.0.6/1) and Project Manager's Checklist (1.1.6/1) to record that this has been done.

QS 1.1	Revision: Date: Written by: P Jackson Reason of issue: Original Authority:	Page 3/3

1.1.6/1 **PROJECT MANAGER'S CHECKLIST**

Job No:	PM:	QD:	(Sign)

Ref:	Action	Complete or N/A	Record	Record Filing
1.1.0	**COMMISSIONING**			
1.1.7	Client's Purchase Order	[ ]	Client's Purchase Order	Job File
1.1.8	Invoicing: Deposit Intermediate	[ ] [ ]	Entry Job Card - 1.1.3/1	Job Card Rack
1.3.0	**JOB PLANNING**			
1.3.1	Job Plan Prepared	[ ]	Job Plan - 1.3.1/1/Equivalent	Job File
1.3.2	Job Plan/Work Card to: Phone Field DP	[ ] [ ] [ ]	Job Plan - 1.3.1/1/Equivalent Work Cards	To Research Units Job File (copy)
1.3.3	Outside Supplier Order	[ ]	Supplier Order - 6.5.6/1	To Supplier/Copy Job File
1.3.4	Commissioning documentation to Client	[ ]		Job File

2.1.0	**PROFESSIONAL RESEARCH**			
2.1.1	Working Papers - Adequately filed	[ ]		
2.1.2	Desk Research - Traceable Source	[ ]		
2.1.3	Discussion/Interview Guides - Record Latest Version No → PM Approved	[ ]	Latest version	Job File
2.1.4	Labelling tapes Labelling transcriptions	[ ] [ ]	Tapes Transcriptions	Working papers
2.1.5	Report of deficient Group recruiting	[ ]	Report deficiency	Job File/Copy to RU Manager
2.1.6	Interview records Contact details & labelling	[ ]	Interview records	Working papers
2.1.7	Incentive records (If incentive given by Researcher/Moderator, etc)	[ ]	Incentive records	Job File/Copy to Accounts

3.1.0	**STRUCTURED INTERVIEWING QUESTIONNAIRES**			
3.1.2	Questionnaire Version - Show latest version →		Latest Version Questionnaire	Job File
3.1.3	Questionnaire Drafter	(Record name)		
3.1.4	PM Check	[ ]		
3.1.5	Client Approval	[ ]		
3.1.6	DP Check	[ ]		
3.1.7	Phone Check	[ ]		
3.1.8	Field Check	[ ]		Note: Field Manager also signs and retains copy
3.1.9	Support Material Check	[ ]		
3.1.10	Field Dispatch Check Received Problems Raised	[ ] [ ]	Note of problems	Job File
3.1.11	Questionnaire Design Review Carried out Report prepared	[ ] [ ]	Report if needed	Job File

205

Ref:	Action		Complete or N/A	Record	Record Filing
3.2.0	**RESEARCH UNIT PLANNING**				
3.2.1	Signed RU Instructions				
		Phone	[ ]	Instructions	
		Field	[ ]	Instructions	To RU's/Copy to Job File
		DP	[ ]	Forms 4.1.1/1, 4.1.1./3	
3.2.2	Sub-contracting: Supplier Order		[ ]	Supplier Order - 6.5.6/1	To supplier/Copy to Job File
3.2.3	Postal Research (Not organised by RU)		[ ]	Form 3.2.3/1	Job File
3.2.4	Piloting:				
		Instructions to RU	[ ]	As 3.2.1	Job File
		Review results	[ ]	Notes	Job File
		Questionnaire revision	[ ]	As 3.1	
		Supplementary RU instructions	[ ]	As 3.2.1	Job File
		Use of completed pilots	[ ]	Notes	Job File
3.3.7	Receive Progress/Problem Report from Phone		[ ]	Report	Job File
3.3.10	Phone Contact Records R'cd		[ ]	Form 3.3.10/2	Job File
3.3.11	Group Respondent Details R'cd		[ ]	Report or questionnaires	Working papers
3.3.17	Receive Phone Unit Completion Report		[ ]	Form 3.3.17/1	Job File
3.4.1	Receive Field Confirmation		[ ]	Form 3.4.1/1	Job File
3.4.4	Venue Details Received		[ ]	Report	Job File
3.4.7	Receive Progress/Problem Report from Field		[ ]	Report	Job File
3.4.16	Report of unsatisfactory Field backcheck		[ ]	Report	Job File
3.4.19	Receive Field Completion Report		[ ]	Form 3.4.19/1	Job File
4.2.2	Coding Frame checked/signed		[ ]	Coding Frames	Return DP
4.3.7	Table checking		[ ]	Tables	Working papers/return DP

5.1.0	**REPORTING**			
5.1.1	Authors	(Record Name)		
5.1.2	Report labelling	[ ]	Report	Report file
5.1.3	PM check	[ ]	Master copy of report signed	Report file
5.1.5	No written report	[ ]		
5.2.0	**PRESENTATIONS**			
5.2.1	PM check	[ ]	Presentation material	Working papers
5.3.0	**JOB COMPLETION**			
5.3.1	Final invoicing	[ ]	Entry Job Card	Job Card Rack
5.3.2	Supplier appraisal	[ ]	Supplier Order Forms	Job File

ALL RELEVANT PROCEDURES FOLLOWED -	
Signed: . . . . (PM)	Date: . . . .
COMPLETED JOB FILE TO SYSTEM ADMINISTRATOR	

PROCEDURE 7.2

INTERNAL QUALITY AUDIT

Purpose

To define procedures relevant to internal auditing of the Procedures.

Scope

All Procedures.

References

The Quality Manual
Procedure Manual   7.3   7.4

Definitions

Internal Quality Audit   An activity, carried out by members of the Company's staff, independent of the area under review, which examines the compliance of the area with Procedures.

Documentation

Register of Audits: 7.2.2/1
Schedule of Audits: 7.2.3/1
Audit Report: 7.2.4/1
Follow-up Audit Report: 7.2.5/1

QS 7.2	Revision: Date: Written by: P Jackson Reason of issue: Original Authority:	Page 1/4

Procedures

7.2.1   Internal Quality Audit Team

The Quality Manager shall appoint persons to act as an Internal Quality Audit Team (IQAT).

The IQAT at any time, shall consist of at least two persons.

The Quality Manager may be one member of the IQAT.

The Quality Manager shall ensure members of the IQAT are adequately trained and prepare and file reports of such training.

7.2.2   IQAT Meetings

When the Quality Manager considers it necessary, he/she shall convene a meeting of the current IQAT to:

•   Review progress to date in IQAs

•   Assign audits by reference to departments of the Company or specific procedures. The audits carried out shall be numbered sequentially and details recorded in the Register Of Audits 7.2.2/1

•   Assess IQAT performance and training needs

7.2.3   Frequency and Coverage of Audits

Over a full year, all parts of the Quality System shall be audited at least once. To ensure this is achieved, the Quality Manager shall prepare in January of each year a Schedule of Audits (using form 7.2.3/1) for the year.

At least one IQA shall be carried out in every quarter of the year.

QS 7.2	Revision: Date: Written by: P Jackson Reason of issue: Original Authority:	Page 2/4

7.2.4   Audit Activities

On receipt of an audit assignment, the auditor shall review the records of audits carried out in the previous twelve months and prepare an audit plan.

The auditor shall arrange a convenient time for the audit with members of staff involved in the relevant working areas subject to the audit.

The audit plan shall detail departments of the Company and specific procedures to be audited.

The audit plan shall be submitted to the Quality Manager or a Quality Director for further recommendations and approval. When approved and signed by the Quality Manager (or Quality Director), the IQAT shall give copies of the audit plan to all departments covered by the audit.

The auditor shall carry out the audit, record findings on the audit plan (7.2.4/2) and prepare an Auditor's Report. The IQAT shall discuss the results with the Quality Manager who shall, where appropriate, issue and have the auditor complete Corrective Action Request Forms (see 7.3) and Change Proposal Forms (see 7.4) which shall lead to the actions defined in 7.3 and 7.4.

The auditors shall make a note on any Quality File consulted in auditing work that the file has been examined. The note shall be in the form:
'Audit No 'X' - Signed: (Auditor)'

The auditor shall complete an Audit Report (7.2.4/1) and pass this to the Quality Manager.

The date the report is received by the Quality Manager shall be entered in the Register Of Audits 7.2.2/1.

All departments covered by the Audit shall receive a copy of the Auditor's Report.

Qs 7.2	Revision: Date: Written by: P Jackson Reason of issue: Original Authority:	Page 3/4

7.2.5   <u>Follow-Up Audit</u>

If as a result of an audit, Corrective Action Request Forms are issued to an auditor, a follow-up audit shall be carried out within 45 days of the date of the Quality Manager receiving Form 7.3.1/1 from the Investigator (see 7.3.5). If a follow-up audit is required the Quality Manager shall assign the task to a member of the IQAT.

The purpose of the follow-up audit shall be to determine in the case of each relevant Corrective Action Request Form whether the Corrective Action raised has been acted upon or not.

A report of the follow-up audit shall be prepared using Form 7.2.5/1 and passed to the Quality Manager.

If the follow-up audit finds that the Corrective Actions raised in the initial audit have been acted upon, it is 'Complete' - the Quality Manager shall record the date the follow-up was carried out (and the Corrective Actions found to be 'Complete') in the Register of Audits (7.2.2/1).

If the follow-up audit finds that any of the Corrective Actions raised in the initial audit has not been acted upon, it is 'Incomplete'. The Quality Manager, at his discretion, shall consider raising an additional Corrective Action, in which case the follow-up audit procedure (as above) will be repeated.

QS 7.2	Revision: Date: Written by: P Jackson Reason of issue: Original Authority:	Page 4/4

7.2.2/1   **REGISTER OF AUDITS**

AUDIT No	DATE STARTED	AUDIT COVERAGE	AUDITOR	DATE REPORT RECEIVED	DATE FOLLOW-UP AUDIT

7.2.3/1   SCHEDULE OF AUDITS

AUDIT NO	PLANNED DATE	COVERAGE

7.2.4/1   **AUDIT REPORT**

AUDIT NUMBER:	DEPARTMENT AUDITED:	DATE OF AUDIT:
FOR SCOPE OF AUDIT SEE ATTACHED COPY OF AUDIT PLAN		
Number of non-conformities		
Report of non-conformities		
Auditee's comments		
Any problems experienced		
Any further comments or recommendations from audit team		

Signed: _____ (Auditors)

_____ Date:

Copies to:

RESULT OF AUDIT:	
Corrective Action Number(s):	Change Proposal Number(s):

Quality in Market Research

7.2.5/1   FOLLOW-UP AUDIT REPORT

Audit No:	Department/Procedure Audited	Date of Audit	Date of Report

Corrective Action Form Number	Satisfactory	Unsatisfactory

FINDINGS/COMMENTS:

AUDITORS: DATE:

214

References and further reading

1 INTRODUCTION

Callingham, M and Smith, G (1994) 'Quality comes to the market research world', *The Journal of the Market Research Society*, 36(4)

Collins, M (1989) 'Concepts of accuracy in market research', Seminar proceedings, Market Research Society, London

Crosby, P (1979) *Quality Is Free*, McGraw-Hill, New York

Deming, W E (1989) *Out of Crisis*, MIT Centre, Cambridge, MA

Ishikawa, K (1985) *What Is Quality Control?*, Prentice-Hall, Englewood Cliffs, NJ

Juran, J M (1989) *Juran on Leadership for Quality*, Free Press, New York

King Taylor, L (1992) *Total Customer Service*, Century Business, London

Smith, D and Dexter, A (1994) 'Quality in market research: hard frameworks for soft problems', *Journal of the Market Research Society*, 36(2)

2 MARKET RESEARCH AS AN INDUSTRY

Deming, W E (1989) *Out of Crisis*, MIT Centre, Cambridge, MA

3 QUALITY AND TRUTH

Admap (1996) Issue 368 – various articles on modelling

Alt, M and Brighton, M (1981) 'Analysing data: or telling stories?', *Journal of the Market Research Society* 23(4)

Belson, A (1986) *Validity in Survey Research*, Gower, London

Brown, S (1995) 'Postmodern marketing research', *Journal of the Market Research Society* 37(3)

Collins, M (1989) 'Concepts of accuracy in market research', Seminal proceedings, Market Research Society, London

Colwell, J (1990) 'Qualitative research', *Journal of the Market Research Society* 32(1)

Cooper, P and Braithwaite, A (1977 'Qualitative technology', *MRS Conference Papers 1977*, Market Research Society, London

Gabriel, C (1990) 'The validity of qualitative research', *Journal of the Market Research Society*, 32(4)

Hague, P (1993) *Questionnaire Design*, Kogan Page, London

Hammersley, M (1993) *Social Research – Philosophy and Practice*, Sage Publications, London

Lawrence, R J (1982) 'To hypothesize or not to hypothesize', *Journal of the Market Research Society*, 24(4)

O'Brien, J (1987) 'Two answers are better than one', *Journal of the Market Research Society*, 29(3)

O'Shaughnessy, J and Holbrook, M B (1988) 'Understanding consumer behaviour: the linguistic turn', *Journal of the Market Research Society*, 30(2)

Popper, K (1959) *The Logic of Scientific Discovery*, Hutchinson and Co, London

Robson, S and Hedges, A (1993) 'Analysis and interpretation of qualitative findings', *Journal of the Market Research Society*, 35(1)

Rothman, J and Mitchell, D (1989) 'Statisticians can be creative too', *Journal of the Market Research Society*, 31(4)

Sayer, A (1992) *Method in Social Science – A Realist Approach*, Routledge, London

Sykes, W (1990) 'Validity and reliability in market research', *Journal of the Market Research Society*, 32(3)

4 QUALITY AND THE PROFESSION

Illich, I et al (1977) *Disabling Professions*, Marion Boyars, London

Lewis, J F (1988) 'Computer expertise and manipulation of knowledge in the market research industry', *Journal of the Market Research Society*, 30(4)

Moore, W E (1970) *The Professions: Roles and Rules*, Russell Sage, New York

MRS (1996) *Code of Conduct*, MRS, London

O'Brien, J (1987) 'Two answers are better than one', *Journal of the Market Research Society*, 29(3)

Rittenburg, T L and Murdock, G W (1994) 'The pros and cons of certifying marketing researchers'. *Marketing Research*, 6(2)

5 QUALITY AND BUSINESS PROCESS

Bendell, T, Kelly, J, Merry, T and Sims, F (1993) *Quality: Measuring and Monitoring*, Century Business, London

Blyth, B and Piper, H (1994) 'Speech recognition – a new dimension in survey research', *Journal of the Market Research Society*, 36(3)

Callingham, M and Smith, G (1994) 'Quality comes to the market research world', *Journal of the Market Research Society*, 36(4)

Chapman, R G (1988) 'False economies in survey research', *Applied Marketing Research*, 28(1)

Klose, A and Ball, A D (1995) 'Using optical mark read surveys', *Journal of the Market Research Society*, 37(3)

Rust, R T and Cooil, B (1994) 'Reliability measures for qualitative data', *Journal of Marketing Research*, 31

6 QUALITY ASSURANCE AND ISO 9000

MRQSA (1995) *Guidelines for the Translation of ISO 9000*, MRQSA, London

7 ISO 9000 – IN MORE DETAIL

British Standards Institution (1994) *BS EN ISO 9001*, BSi, London

Jackson, P and Ashton, D (1993) 'Implementing Quality Through BS 5750', Kogan Page, London

Jackson, P and Ashton, D (1995a) *Achieving BS EN ISO 9000*, Kogan Page, London

Jackson, P and Ashton, D (1995b) *Managing a Quality System Using BS EN ISO 9000*, Kogan Page, London

MRQSA (1995) *Guidelines for the Translation of ISO 9000*, MRQSA, London

8 STANDARDS FOR DATA COLLECTION – IQSC

Kiecker, P and Nelson, J E (1996) 'Do interviewers follow telephone survey instructions?', *Journal of the Market Research Society*, 38(2)

MRS (1996) 'Qualitative recruitment. Report of the Industry Working Party', *Journal of the Market Research Society*, 38(2)

9 STANDARDS FOR THE WHOLE RESEARCH PROCESS – MRQSA

MRQSA (1996) *Services Standards for Market Research Services*, MRQSA, London

MRS (1983) *Guide to Good Coding Practice*, MRS, London
Owen, D (1991) 'Every coding is another encoding', *Journal of the Market Research Society*, 33(4)

10   PEOPLE QUALITY – INVESTORS IN PEOPLE

Investors in People Unit (1993) *Investors in People Standard*, IiP Unit, London

11   QUALITY AND INTERNATIONAL RESEARCH

Mytton, G (1996) 'Research in new fields', *Journal of the Market Research Society*, 38(1)
Owen, D (1991) 'Every coding is another encoding', *Journal of the Market Research Society*, 33(4)
Taylor, H (1995) 'Horses for courses', *Journal of the Market Research Society*, 37(3)
Weitz, J (1989) 'Quality standards for the single market', *Marketing and Research Today*, November 1989

12   DEVELOPING A QUALITY SYSTEM

Jackson, P and Ashton, D (1995) *Managing a Quality System Using BS EN ISO 9000*, Kogan Page, London

Index

ABMRC 30, 142, 153
accountancy 17, 69, 155
Accounting Standards Board 70
ad hoc research 22, 26, 34, 77, 99,
  154
after sales 22
Alt, M 47, 54
AMSO 28, 142, 153
ancillary workers 58
anonymous data 28
appraisal 142, 144
approved assessors 198
approved suppliers 119
AQRP 64, 153
Ashton, D 114, 130
assessment 17, 132–4, 146–7, 162–4,
  175–6, 198
assessment costs 163
assessment indicators 173
attitude research 26
auditability 185
auditable procedures 107
auditing 88, 129, 195, 197–8
AURA 30, 142, 153, 154
authentication 62

back checking 103, 145
Ball, A D 81

Belson, A 52
benchmarking 90
Bendell, T 83
Blyth, B 81
Braithwaite, A 50
brief 77
Brighton, M 47, 54
British Quality Foundation 92
British Standards 89, 152, 164
British Telecom 66
Brotherhood 60
Brown, S 49
BS 5750 *see* ISO 9000
BSI 152, 16
BSI Quality Assurance 166
Business and Industrial Group 63
business planning 77
business plans 174
business to business research 52
buyer reassurance 165

calling 60
Callingham, M 12, 77
Cantar 180
capability 20
CAPI 23, 36, 52, 81, 82, 145, 161, 169
CATI 23, 52, 81, 82,140, 145, 161,
  169

Index

caveat emptor 15
CEN 181
certification 61, 108
charting 188–90
cheating 138–9
checklists 196
closed professions 59
closing out 129
code frame 161
Code of Conduct 65, 99, 159
coding 82, 160, 161
Collins, M 14, 40, 50, 54
Colwell, J 49
combined assessment 162
commitment 19, 109, 167, 172, 174, 188
competitive advantage 77
computer files 161
conceptualisation 45
confidence 77
confidentiality 68
consistency 54
consultants 188
continuous assessment 133, 163
continuous research 22, 26, 34, 54
contract review 99, 117
contracts 97
controlled copies 197
Cooil, B 81
Cooper, P 50
corrective action 103, 128
cottage industry 137
courses 170
creativity 98
Crosby, P 12, 13
cross auditing 130
cultural differences 178
customer satisfaction 12
customer supplied products 119

data analysis 32, 34
data collection 32, 82, 160
data comparisons 178
data dredging 47, 48
data entry 160, 161
data preparation 35
data processing 82, 160–2

Data Protection Act 66
Data Protection Agency 28
data testing 53
database marketing 66, 68
decision making 40
deduction 43
Defence Standard 95
delighting customers 79
delivery 21, 22
Deming W E 12, 35, 104
Department of Training 172
description 48
design 20, 96–8, 114–17
design changes 117
design control 114
development 170
Dexter, A 24
division of labour 80
document control 128, 187, 195
documentation 126

editing 145, 160
education 17
EFEMRA 181
efficiency 80
electronic files 107
empowerment 90
EN 29000 95
error reduction 82
ESOMAR 181, 184
ethics 60
evaluation 171
excellence 13, 22, 73, 75
executive standards 158–60
executives 33
experiment 43, 47
explanation 49

field and tab 31, 96
field interviewing 136
filing 107, 196
financial performance 79
Financial Reporting Standards 17
Formatting 187
forms 105, 196
fraud 148
full service 31

Gabriel, C 49
generalisation 53
GIMRA 63
guidelines 68

Hague, P 50
Hammersley, M 42, 47
handling 122
Hedges, A 50
hermeneutics 49
hierarchies 43
historical analysis 49
Holbrook, M B 49
humanistic research 49
hypothesis 41, 43, 47
hypothetico-deductive logic 39, 43, 48

ICS 141
identity cards 141, 146
Illich, I 60, 72
implementation 132, 164, 174
IMRA 63
induction 43, 48
informants 66
Infratest Burke 180
initial assessment 133
inspection 120, 21, 87, 88, 102, 146–7
inspection and test status 121
International Broadcasting Audience Research 180
Internal audits 103
Internal consistency 52
Internal customers 90
International standards 108
interviewer variability 138, 145
interviewers 35
interviewing 135–141
Initial assessment 162
Investors in People 19, 90, 101, 172
involvement of staff 169
IPSOS 180
IQCS 11, 18, 21, 36, 88, 89, 94, 102, 103, 179, 181, 184
ISBA 153, 154
Ishikawa, K 12
ISO 181

ISO 9000 11–24, 89, 93–111, 151–4, 174, 183
IT 23, 36, 52, 81

Jackson, P J 114, 130
job numbers 107, 196
Juran, J M 12

Kiecker, P 140
King Taylor, L 18
Kitemark 18, 89
Klose, A 81
knowledge 61–3

labour costs 81
laity 34, 71
language barriers 178
Lawrence, R J 48
learned societies 64
least cost 13, 79
Lewis, J F 61
linguistic turn 49

malpractice 36, 138–9
management representative 105, 129
management responsibility 125
management review 104–5
manufacturing industry 87
market analysis 26
marketing 20
measuring and testing equipment 123
media research 26
methodology 26, 31, 40, 68
minimum standards 165
mission 18
Mitchell, D 53
models 45
monitoring 103, 140
monopolies 59
Moore, W E 57
MQA 166
MRQSA 11, 36, 89, 93, 94, 98, 102, 103, 114, 142, 181, 183, 184, 188, 195
MRS 23, 32, 33, 57, 62, 63, 141, 142, 153, 170, 184
MRS Diploma 64

Murdock, G W 62
mystery shopping 26, 140
Mytton, G 180

natural history 48
needs 14, 71
Nelson, J E 140
new product development 26
Nielsen 180
nominalism 42
non-conforming products 122
numbering systems 186
NVQs 64, 170, 173

O'Brien, J 52, 62
O'Shaughnessy, J 49
on-screen procedures 187
open professions 59
ordering frameworks 45
Owen, D 179

packaging 122
paradigm 45
Pareto 30
PECS 166
peer group 23
phenomenalism 42
phone interviewing 140
Piper, H 81
Popper, K 42, 43
portfolio of evidence 175
positivism 39, 42
post modernism 49
prediction 47
preventive action 103, 128
primary research 26
problem solving 99, 103
procedure manual 106
procedure planning 188
procedures 127, 184–96
process 20, 85
process control 100, 118
product identification 107
production 21
productivity 80, 81
professional codes 28, 63, 65, 71
professional constitution 63, 65

professional education 61
professional ethics 121
professional responsibility 83, 110
professional status 71
professionalism 14, 15, 19, 57
professions 33
programming 160
project checklists 106
project control 99
project management 99, 118, 161
proof of research 55
proposals 97
proprietary research 32, 96
purchasing 102, 119, 195

qualitative research 31, 54, 48–50
quality assurance 83, 88, 93–111,
    156–8, 183
quality circles 90
quality control 83
quality improvements 198
quality manual 106, 126, 196
quality measurement 83
quality plans 106, 127
quality records 124
quality system 88, 126
quality system circle 130
quality system control 125–32
quantitative research 31
questionnaires 50

rates of pay 137
receiving inspection 102, 121
records 68, 142
re-engineering 12, 19, 92
relative quality 13, 22, 75
reliability 39, 50–55
repeatability 54
requirements 98–9
requirements of ISO 9000 113–14
Research 168
research design 42
research industry 25
research tools 23
resources 101
respondent cooperation 37
respondent qualification 52

responsibility 186
retail auditing 32
reviews 116, 173
rhetoric 42, 76
Rittenburg, T L 62
Robson, S 50
Rothman, J 53
Rust, R T 81

sales 42
Sayer, A 45
secondary research 26
self-regulation 59
semiotics 49
service delivery 76
Service Standard for Market Research 153
servicing 122
SGS Yarsley 166
signing-off 185
skill audit 169
skills 167, 169
Smith, A 80
Smith, D 24
Smith, G 12, 77
social science 42
social survey 26
Sofres 180
sole practitioners 58
special processes 103
specialisation 31, 58
specification 78–79
specing 160
SRA 153
standardisation 180
standards 15, 16, 185, 195
statistical techniques 124
storage 122
sugging 66, 141
supervisors 136

supplier evaluation 119
SVQs 173
Sykes, W 50, 54
system changes 195
system launch 196
system management 195

Taylor, H 178
Taylor Nelson AGB 30
team building 90
team working 80
TECs 172, 174, 176
telemarketing 66
testing 21, 88, 102, 120
testing procedures 196
theory 45, 48
TQM 12, 19, 22, 83, 89, 103, 110
training 101, 123, 137, 138, 142–4, 168, 185, 195
translation 179
translation documents 94
truth 14, 39, 50

UKAS 133, 162
understanding 47, 48–50
usefulness 14, 40

validation 117, 142, 144–5, 148
validity 39, 50–5
value free 42
value of research 28
variability 52
variance 36
verification 103, 116
vision 172

wants 14, 76
Weitz, J 181
work instructions 106, 127
WPP 180